# BREAKTHROUGH

## *Becoming Intimate with God*

# BREAKTHROUGH

*Becoming Intimate with God*

## How to Listen to the Lord

Sara Trollinger

## Praise for *Breakthrough*

*"No matter what, your past is your past, but you can learn from it. You have to hear how God wants to change your present and improve your future."*

—Brianna, a resident at House of Hope

*"Before I read your book, I was way too busy to get quiet and listen for His direction. While trying to get my business up and running, I just* **expected** *Him to be with me all day long. Breakthrough helped me realize that I was taking Him for granted. Now I eagerly look forward to my morning meetings with Him. I can tell you that the little things don't bother me nearly as much. I have more patience. I can find all kinds of reasons to praise Him when things don't flow easily. This was the refresher course that I needed. 'Get back to the basics...and stay there!'"*

—Dr. Maureen Haner, Sanford, FL

*"I really enjoyed reading the book Breakthrough written by Sara Trollinger. I had been talking to my wife about hearing from God. My wife encouraged me to read this book. I followed what it said, I asked God to convict me of any sin that was in my life and I confessed my sins to God. As the book told me, I bound Satan and cast him into the deepest pit of hell by the authority given to me by Jesus. I read the Bible and sang praises to God. I asked the Lord to speak to me. I felt God speaking to me in His still small voice. I felt loved and comforted by God. I would highly recommend others to read this book."*

— Don McCoy, father of
House of Hope resident Matthew

*I have known Sara for many years and have always admired the strength of her faith. Breakthrough is a wonderful book that shares personal insight into Sara's faith through her "listening time" with the Lord."*

—Steve Cahill, President Cahill Homes,
Orlando, FL

**An excerpt from the preface of**
***Speak, Lord...for Your Servant is Listening***

*"I came away from a class taught by Sara Trollinger entitled "How to Listen to the Lord" feeling very preoccupied! What if what she was saying really worked? Could we honestly still expect God to speak to us individually as He spoke to the prophets of old? The possibilities were exciting! I could hardly wait to get home and see if it worked for me! I made sure I had fulfilled the conditions outlined in her talk...there was no one I needed to forgive, Jesus truly was the Lord of my life, I made sure I was repentant for any sins in my past, and I truly desired to seek Him above all else. Okay, my motives were right. With pen in hand, and note pad ready, I said, "Okay, Lord, I'm ready...if you are." I began to write!*

*That was the beginning of it all for me. After thirty years of writing words the Lord gave me each morning, I was urged by the Lord, and by so many who had been blessed by those messages to pick some and put into a book I called* Speak, Lord...for Your Servant Is Listening.

*Thank you, my precious friend, Sara, for beginning what has turned out to be such a blessing to so many...thousands have read Speak Lord and have been blessed, many lives have been transformed because of those anointed words from the Lord...and all because of the tremendous impact Sara's Breakthrough has had on my life, so much so that I am now finishing* A Light Unto My Path *which is a continuation of these messages. Isn't that just like the Lord?"*

—Carol Wagner Brown, author and teacher

Scripture quotations identified RSV are taken from the Revised Standard Version of the Bible.

Scripture quotations identified KJV are from the King James Version of the Bible.

Scripture quotations identified NKJV are from the New King James Version of the Bible.

Scripture quotations identified TM are from The Message version of the Bible.

Scripture quotations identified CEV are from the Contemporary English Version of the Bible

Scripture quotations identified NLT are from the New Living Translation Version of the Bible.

Scripture quotations identified TNIV are from The New International Version of the Bible.

Names have been changed throughout this book to protect privacy.



Cover design by Eric Wilbanks.



Published in the United States
by HigherLife Press
2342 Westminster Terrace
Oviedo, FL 32765

ISBN: 0-9793227-0-7
978-0-9793227-0-7

This book was previously published as ***Breakthrough***: How to Listen to the Lord – A Handbook by Fellowship of Faith Ministry, Inc., copyright 1981, revised 1993

**Lovingly Dedicated to:**

My precious Mother and Daddy
whose lives were a godly example—
and to all the boys, girls, and
staff at all the Houses of Hope across America

# Table of Contents

## Part Two
## The Practical Side of Listening

# Preface

There are millions of wounded and hurting teenagers in America today. Not all of them are hanging out on the street corners, living in abandoned junk cars, running drugs, or prostituting themselves. They look like any kid next door but they are out of control, rebellious, and on a collision course with self-destruction. That is until they walk in the front door of House of Hope.

Sara Trollinger had a dream and a few hundred dollars in her pocket. There was no doubt in her mind that she had heard God's voice and direction. She chose to obey and trust that He would provide for these troubled kids. He did not let her down.

She knows their struggles first hand as she sees it every day in her ever-widening healing ministry where she works with teens at the House of Hope in Orlando, a proven and successful model and pattern for more than fifty other residential facilities across the nation.

Her unique and personal relationship and deep-rooted experiences of more than forty years with the God of grace and mercy she found at a Billy Graham crusade has paved the way for her passion. She received her bachelor's degree from the University of North Carolina, her master's degree from the University of South Florida and has worked with emotionally handicapped young people for more than four decades.

The success of House of Hope cannot be measured. The lives that have been touched and changed, families that have been reunited, residents that have gone on to become loving parents and responsible members of society is a number that is incalculable...but God knows. He smiles and continues to bless House of Hope every day because this is His will and His heart.

> "And he will turn the hearts of the fathers to the children, and the hearts of the children to their fathers, lest I come and strike the earth with a curse."
> —Malachi 4:6 (NKJV)

Sara has devoted her life to breaking those curses that cause family collapse.

# Introduction

I believe we can sit in a church pew Sunday after Sunday, sing the songs, pray the prayers, listen to every word the preacher says, pay our tithes, live a good life, and still miss God's voice and His direction for our lives. God wants to speak to His children, but it's up to us to seek His presence and learn to hear His voice.

The story is told of a dear saint who died and went to heaven. God gave him a tour of heaven...all except for one room...that door he did not open.

"You've shown me every room except that room," the dear old saint exclaimed.

"You could not stand to look in that room, God replied, "because in there are all the things that you **could** have had if only you had known how to listen to Me for direction and guidance. Psalm 2:8 (NKJV) says, "Ask of Me, and I will give *You* the nations *for* Your inheritance, and the ends of the earth *for* Your possession."

# Let's get real...

- **Is there an area in your life that you have ignored, not cleaned up, or surrendered?**
- **Do you have questions that you are embarrassed or afraid to ask God?**

Have you been searching for answers, and in your searching turned to other sources? Or, like Job, have you turned to well-meaning friends? Maybe you have even tried the occult? Have you dialed the number on television hoping to find answers from psychics? Have you gone for professional help before looking to the Lord for your answers? Or maybe in desperation, you have begun searching within yourself for the answers.

In your zest and zeal to know God, have you found yourself spending your time tracking down popular speakers, attending countless meetings, listening to every Christian tape you could find? Do you stay so busy with "stuff" that you feel frustrated? If you can answer yes to any of those questions, you are probably uncomfortable getting alone and quietly listening for His voice. Sure, you want to experience it, but you just cannot stop the world long enough to get still and have quiet time. Do not give up or lose hope!

There comes a time in our spiritual growth when we want to hear **from** God rather than just to hear **about** Him. We need to be alone with Him in order to listen and hear what He has to say to us. His desire is to deal with each one of us directly and personally. Our communication must be two-way. Our songs of praise, our prayers, and even our tears, are happily accepted by Him, but this is only one-way communication. This is from us to Him. Now learn how to hear His voice when you call upon Him...*and listen.*

In my experience with the teens, it generally does not take them long to make that eighteen inch journey from head knowledge to an understanding in their hearts. I love to watch their reactions and see their faces light up with astonishment after they have heard from God for the first time. It is a touching "ah-ha" moment in each person's life. To preserve that moment, I encourage them to record the words in journals so they never forget. This is just a first step on their journey to wholeness and happiness.

Every Wednesday I spend an hour with the boys and an hour with the girls in the program. We call the time "Fireside Chats." Here in Florida we do not have a fireplace but we do lots of chatting, sharing testimonies, teaching, and learning how to be still and listen to the Lord.

Just recently I shared with them that God loves them and has so much He wants to say to them. After a short teaching all were separated and sent into a quiet place to listen to the Lord. After almost twenty minutes, we came back together to share what God had said. Everyone (except two) was filled with amazement at what God shared with each of them.

These are some of God's messages to the teenagers:

- "Now is the time for you to forgive your parents and all those who have hurt you."
- "I know it's hard for you to trust, but I will not harm you."
- "I am setting you free from drugs."

Wouldn't you like to know the contents of your room behind the closed door? How would your life have been different if you had "heavenly foresight"? Never again, after reading this book, will you need to wonder what God's advice is in any area of your life. You will know how to seek Him and find the answers by listening for your own personal message.

Breakthrough! The decision is yours…you may listen to God…and have His answers, or you may choose to follow your own path. I firmly believe that your life is getting ready to take on a whole new dimension. Your spiritual life is going to expand in a mighty way as you discover your own private "BREAKTHROUGH."

# Prologue

Before the first printing of *Breakthrough,* I had about a seven-year "listening relationship" with the Lord. He told me during my listening time several years ago about specific areas that I should follow in developing House of Hope for hurting teenage girls between the ages of twelve and eighteen. Not only did He give me the name for this ministry, "House of Hope," but through the years He has given me specifics about building the staff and the board. God has told me what to expect in business and my personal life as well. He also told me House of Hope would receive national attention long before President and Mrs. Reagan came to House of Hope. He told me House of Hope would be a model for other ministries across the nation. I have included excerpts from some of these private listening times with the Lord, which at the time seemed impossible. Many of these listening times have already been fulfilled and other things the Lord told me continue to unfold.

The story of House of Hope has been included in the last section of this book. How exciting to have God share with me, and then see the things He told me become a reality!

I want to encourage you to spend daily intimate time with Him. Dig into His Word and listen to what He wants to tell you. Be sure to write down what He says to you and keep your listenings to refer to later.

## Let's get real...

- **When is the last time you had quiet time—without asking God for anything?**
- **Is there something deep inside of you that longs for a better spiritual connection?**
- **Have you ever thought or said, "Why can't I have her kind of faith?"**

God has no favorites! What He does for me He'll do for you. "*Jesus Christ* is *the same yesterday, today, and forever.*" (Hebrews 13:8 NKJV)

# PART ONE

# Preparing for Intimacy for God

Chapter 1

# If You Have Ears...

Oh, the excitement of hearing a message from the Lord and then, in awe, watching as it unfolds and becomes a reality...even when well-meaning friends may say, "But Sara, that's impossible. Are you sure you heard from the Lord? It's just not realistic!" Yet inside, I know that I know, because He told me so.

## Listeners of the Past

Years ago during one of my quiet times, the Lord told me that not only would I lead a fellowship group, but the group would have over seventy members and that He would give the increase. He knew my mind, which was already analyzing, and justifying, "But Lord, I don't want a fellowship group...who would come? But Lord...I live in a condominium—it would never hold all those people if everyone came."

It was as if He said, "Never mind the details, I have it all worked out." So I wrote it down in my listening notebook and forgot it. I cannot thank the Lord enough for teaching me to write down my "listenings," for in the stressful times of developing this fellowship group (and in every project there are stressful times), rereading what He told me gave me great comfort and the confidence to go on.

Incidentally, the group did reach seventy-five members, and He did help me find a larger place to meet that accommodated everyone. Not only did He choose the people, but it was a delight to stand and watch how He worked in their lives as they began to show signs of spiritual growth and leadership.

Several years of listening have brought similar words which the Lord has shared with me. Some have been words of knowledge, wisdom, various words of comfort, admonitions, and yes, even many chastisements!

I haven't always had this kind of relationship with the Lord. It has only been this way since I learned to listen to Him. I find He is always ready to talk to me when I am willing to spend time with Him. He is always right there...waiting.

Today, as in no other time in history, God is trying to get our attention. We are being prepared for the great event that is about to take place. Jesus is coming for His believers and the rapture is not far away. There is much that God wants to say to us about all of this. We are the actors in these events and we must know how to play our role. Time is getting short. The scene is being prepared. The curtain is about to go up! Our spirits need to be listening for promptings from the Lord, our director. We need last minute instructions and cues!

For a long time God has been trying to bring us to a point where He could get our attention. He wants to speak to us today right where we are. He has been trying to tell us things for a long time, yet we fail to quit talking and become quiet long enough to hear what He has to say. He has been patiently waiting for us to see Him.

How many times have you charged into a situation, armed with your own limited knowledge, only to find yourself in a state of remorse and regret? I know that I have done that. Then, later, we ask ourselves, "What went wrong?" If only we had known how to listen to what the Lord had to say about it!

Let me share an example from my own experience. In the early days of House of Hope, there were many pregnant teenagers and we were taking calls day and night. Many people suggested that we open one of the three houses just for pregnant teens. We did exactly that!

In preparation, we sent out press releases to the media, contacted all the local and state officials, and even had the governor come for the ribbon-cutting ceremony. We hosted a huge reception and were given all kinds of encouragement and verbal support. The doors opened but the phone calls stopped. Finally, our first pregnant teenager arrived.

No one could have ever guessed what kind of chaos she would bring to the program. She demanded special privileges, broke all the rules, showered in the middle of the night, craved chocolate morning, noon, and night, and needed special freedoms that were not permitted to the other girls. With all the special attention, the other girls decided they wanted to get pregnant.

For weeks, no more calls came in and we were all praying and listening to the Lord. Finally, He said, ***"I never called you to start a teenage pregnancy center. I want you to stay focused on your calling—to help hurting teens."***

## Let's get real...

- **How many times have you bowed to the seemingly "good" suggestions of others?**
- **What did you learn when you finally discovered that you had stepped outside of God's plan for you?**
- **What blessings did you miss while you were doing your own thing?**
- **Can you tell when God's anointing has lifted from you? How do you feel?**

I have found that doing things my way—even to fill a kingdom need—is not always God's way. During that "stalled out" time, we turned away many teenagers who needed our help. I know that He lifted the anointing from our program and it certainly got my attention. The financial blessings halted, the program lost its focus, and even worse, I felt separated from my Father. I felt alone and cut off from Him. I got ahead of Him and I paid a price!

This really is much like being in the military. You simply cannot be a part-time officer. You cannot take or give commands one day, and the next day ignore them and go off and do your own thing. You must be willing to surrender to authority in order to survive and to protect others in your care. Whether it is family, friends, students, patients, or strangers that God brings your way, you cannot be a part-time Christian. You are either moving forward or you are sliding back. There is no neutral in the Kingdom!

Do you want to be part of God's end-time army? You can, if you learn to listen to Him, take orders, and carry out His will. You need to become a disciplined and obedient listener. He wants to speak to you today, just as He spoke to the Old Testament people.

As you read those stories, do you ever wonder if prophets, patriarchs, and others really were just ordinary people as we are today? I suppose God talked to as many people back then as would listen to Him, yet some of those conversations were so life-changing that they were recorded not only as historical fact, but also that we might have examples of listening to His voice after which we can pattern our own listening.

You might be thinking ahead and asking yourself who were some of the great Old Testament listeners, and how did they hear God's voice? Was it a booming voice? Was it an impression? Could everyone hear Him? Or, was it directed to just one person at a time? With this in mind, let's think together about the prophet Moses. God called him to lead a rebellious, sniveling people.

## Moses

Moses was a lowly shepherd boy. He was really nothing special, probably not even noticeable in a crowd. He had few possessions: the rags on his back, a tent and a rod to keep his sheep from straying. He even stuttered. Yet, he was the one through whom God chose to speak, the one who was to lead Israel out of bondage. Moses must have found it hard to believe that God would choose to speak to him, one with such poor qualifications, to lead His chosen people.

Why was Moses chosen? The answer is obvious: He was willing to listen and be obedient to God's Word.

Moses could hardly believe that God was telling him to go before Pharaoh demanding freedom for his people that had been enslaved for years. He listened again. Yes, that was what God was saying to him. Moses began by making excuses for his poor diction and told God to use Aaron as he was quite eloquent in his speech. God said, "You can do it." Moses didn't trust his ears. He didn't believe what he heard. He kept making excuses, but God, in exasperation, said, "Okay. I'll let Aaron do the talking," and then God spoke also to Aaron.

Do you see yourself in Moses' actions? This does get our attention knowing that we can identify with him in his shortcomings, inadequacies, and frailties, and knowing, too, that he was just an ordinary person much like us.

To further prove that God was speaking, He told Moses to put his hand in his tunic. He did and when he pulled it out it was leprous. Moses must have been horrified as he looked at the hand that had held the rod as a shepherd and that now would be an outcast. Then God spoke to him and told him to put his hand inside his tunic again.

Let's stop right here for a moment and think. What a predicament! Moses would have been in serious trouble with that leprous hand if he had not been patient and had not listened as God spoke the second time. Thank God his hand was cleansed and healed and because Moses listened, it became a testimony to God's greatness.

After leading the Hebrews safely across the Red Sea, Moses heard them murmuring discontentedly. He took this to the Lord in prayer because there were too many people to ignore. God shared certain conditions that he was to present to the people and their compliance would prove their level of commitment to Him. We all know what happened.

> He said, "If you will listen carefully to the voice of the LORD your God and do what is right in his sight, obeying his commands and keeping all his decrees, then I will not make you suffer any of the diseases I sent on the Egyptians; for I am the LORD who heals you" (Exodus 15:26 NLT)

How can we receive God's promises if we have not first fulfilled His conditions? The commandment is for us to listen, obey, and then the blessing will follow.

## Noah

Let's change the scene from Moses to Noah. Genesis 6:9b (NLT) says, "Noah was a righteous man, the only blameless person living on earth at the time, and he walked in close fellowship with God." If Noah had not listened, all of God's creatures would have perished.

God expressed regret that He had ever created mankind, who had become so wicked (Genesis 6:6). He confided to Noah His plan to destroy all flesh upon the earth, but Noah found grace in the eyes of the Lord. God gave him detailed instructions for the construction of an ark, which would enable him, his family, and a multitude of living creatures to survive the mighty flood that God was about to release upon the earth. Noah obeyed.

Can't you just see how people must have laughed and scorned him, made fun of him and criticized him? He was probably even called a fanatic! But he followed God's orders to the last detail. As a result of his obedient listening, he and all that were aboard the ark were saved to repopulate the earth.

Noah could have argued with God and protested that the job of building such an enormous vessel would be impractical. He could have denied that it was the voice of God and gone about his own business to his peril, yet he was obedient, and for one hundred and twenty years he preached and built, trying to get mankind to listen.

## Let's get real...

- **Have you ever made fun of someone who was being obedient to God?**
- **Has anyone ever mocked you because of your obedience?**
- **Did their taunts hurt you or motivate you keep going?**

If God were to ask you to undertake a challenge of this magnitude today, what would you do? Would you listen and obey?

## Abraham

What can be said about Abraham, "the father of many nations?" When Abraham was seventy-five years old, God spoke to him and told him that He would lead him into a new land. In Genesis 13:15 (KJV) we read, "...to thee will I give it, and to thy seed [descendants] forever." Can you picture Abraham gathering together his aging wife, Sarah, and his possessions, and following God's leading? One part of God's promise he found hard even to imagine. How could a couple of people at their age have a child? They had no children to call "seed." Nevertheless, he listened and believed God. For another long, twenty-five years he waited for the coming of that promised heir. Imagine his joy when, at the age of one hundred, his ninety-year-old wife gave birth to their promised son, Isaac.

What anguish Abraham must have endured, when God called upon him a few years later to sacrifice his beloved son, Isaac. This was a true test of his obedience. He bound his son to the altar and, as he raised the knife to slay him, he heard the angel of the Lord speaking,

> And He said, "Do not lay your hand on the lad, or do anything to him; for now I know that you fear God, seeing you have not withheld your son, your only *son,* from Me" (Genesis 22:12 NKJV).

God was faithful to His promise. Abraham never stopped listening and believing God. He did become "the father of many nations" as God had promised him.

Maybe you are thinking that you are a has-been! Perhaps you are stuck in a rut where you play those old tapes and hear those old voices telling you that you will never amount to anything because you of your past. God's Word clearly says, forget the past! Isaiah 43:18-19 (CEV) reads, "Forget what happened long ago! Don't think about the past. I am creating something new. There it is! Do you see it? I have put roads in deserts, streams in thirsty lands."

Because this is a new day and because God is doing a new thing, I would like to challenge you. Get on the cutting edge and do not miss what He is saying to you. Will you receive it? He wants to tell you things you need to know. Did you know that He has a phone number? Jeremiah 33:3 (The Message) invites you by saying, "...Call to me and I will answer you. I'll tell you marvelous and wondrous things that you could never figure out on your own."

God is calling out to whoever will listen for His special direction. In Isaiah 6:8 (NKJV), God was not particularly addressing Isaiah, but Isaiah was attuned to God's voice... He had a listening relationship with God. Isaiah was in the presence of God and he overheard the call: "Whom shall I send, and who will go for us?" Isaiah realized there was nothing else for him to do but say, "Here am I! Send me." God is calling all of us who are willing to listen and obey Him. We, too, shall hear God say in that still, small voice, "...This is the way, walk ye in it..." (Isaiah 30:21 KJV).

We can read of the lives of Gideon, Elisha, David, Hezekiah, and many others in the Old Testament who were great listeners. God chose to speak through these men because He could trust them to fulfill His plans. God locked David away in the wilderness to care for his father's sheep. There, the shepherd boy not only learned about worship, intercession, and warfare—he learned to journal.

When you read Psalms, you are really reading David's journal (Psalm 22, 32, 81 etc.).

## Paul

God spoke to His people in the New Testament also. For example, God spoke to Paul (even before he became a believer) and gave him specific directions. In Acts 9 we read about Paul's journey to Damascus, where he was going to continue persecuting the disciples of the Lord. In this chapter we read an exciting account of how the Lord struck Paul blind for three days, changed his name from Saul to Paul, and changed him from being a persecutor of Christians to the man who wrote most of the New Testament. Again in Acts 18 and Acts 28 we read of God speaking to Paul, because Paul had "ears to hear."

Let me share about Stephen, a young man who ***thought*** that he had heard from God and what happened when he did not hold it up to Scripture. He was one of our male house staff who unexpectedly came into the office and resigned. He related how that morning when he was taking a shower, he heard the Lord tell him to quit before he went on duty to take care of eight boys. I reminded him that his year commitment to the position was not complete and if he was to leave, he was to give a two-week notice. I even requested that he go to his pastor for counseling but he felt that his pastor had nothing to do with this decision. He was convinced that God had spoken and given him the order. He walked away. In a few days, he called and offered to come back. By this time he'd already been replaced. What he thought he had heard was not scriptural. He had heard something supernatural—but it was not from God!

Who of our generation can God trust to listen, to carry out His plans, and to fulfill His perfect will? We can observe the outstanding qualities that those biblical characters all shared in common—just ordinary people with listening hearts.

## Let's get real...

- **Do you want a listening heart?**
- **Are you an ordinary person?**
- **Are you thinking, "What can I do?"**

God's Word says that His sheep hear His voice. As His sheep, let's find out what is required of us.

Did you know that there have always been rebellious lambs that would not stay with the flock? They wandered off time after time. What you might not know is that often times the shepherd would go find the lamb and intentionally break its leg. The shepherd would splint the leg and he would carry the lamb around his neck for many weeks while the leg healed. During that time the little lamb had no choice but to hear his voice. When the leg was properly healed, the lamb was put back with the flock and seldom ran off again.

On a more human note, Sergio came to the House of Hope after fifteen years of rejection and hurt. He was full of anger because his father had been in and out of his life and never gave him the kind of home or love he needed and wanted. Sergio showed his hurt through rage and other inappropriate behaviors. He was in and out of serious trouble before he came to our program.

Even after a few months, he would still hit the punching bag until his knuckles bled. There never seemed to be a full release of his pent-up anger. As the days went on, staff and residents were growing deeply concerned for him.

One day Jesus called Sergio's name. Sergio had an encounter with Jesus Christ that changed his life forever. Finally, he discovered that he would never be alone, rejected, or abandoned ever again. There was someone who would always be there for him.

I wish I could tell you that the anger just melted away, but that would not be true. It took time. Sergio had to learn to trust God, but an incredible relationship was built in the process. The healing experience with God helped him find his identity. Today he has great hope, a promising future, and he is fulfilling his destiny.

Chapter 2

# "My Sheep Hear My Voice"

## God Wants Us to Listen Today

The voice of the LORD rolls over the water.
The voice of the LORD is powerful.
The voice of the LORD is majestic.
The voice of the LORD breaks the cedars,
The voice of the LORD strikes with flashes of
  lightening.
The voice of the LORD makes the wilderness
  tremble.
The voice of the LORD splits the oaks
and strips the trees of the forest bare.
Everyone in his temple is saying, "Glory!"

—Psalm 29 (GWT)—selected verses

One of the first things the Lord said to me when I began to listen to His promptings was to spend time with Him, to "be still" and know that He is God. God wants us to come apart daily…to be still…to meditate on His Word...to pray His Word. This is where He reveals Himself. This is where we mature and where we become like Him. In John 15:4 (NKJV) Jesus commands us to abide in Him. "Abide in Me, and I in you. As the branch cannot bear fruit of itself, unless it abides in the vine, neither can you, unless you abide in Me."

There is a wonderful promise linked with this command. Verse 7 (NKJV) goes on to say, "If you abide in Me, and My words abide in you, you will ask what you desire, and it shall be done for you." Jesus went on to say that if we keep His commandments we shall abide in His love. He spoke these things to us that His joy might remain in us and that our joy might be full. What a reward! What a blessing we receive when we get to know His voice and follow His Word!

Was it only a chosen few that heard God's voice thousands of years ago? Are you thinking that God only spoke to the Old Testament Hall of Fame? If there were a present day Hall of Fame, are you willing to be on a listening road that could eventually qualify you to hear from Him? Hebrews 13:8 (NKJV) says, "Jesus Christ *is* the same yesterday, today, and forever." Or perhaps you even think you have to be from a very select group, that you aren't good enough. Do you know that you are? God has no favorites—He loves us all the same.

God isn't choosing the wise, the self-assured, the knowing, or the well-educated. "Instead, God chose things the world considers foolish in order to shame those who think they are wise. And he chose things that are powerless to shame those who are powerful" (1 Corinthians 1:27 NLT). In other words, He is choosing the people who are not arrogant, those who are open to Him, who are not proud, who see themselves as nothing. He is choosing those who are willing to humble themselves and listen.

Once we had a young girl in our program who had been sexually abused by her father. She was withdrawn, did poorly in school, and she would not talk. She was emotionally scarred. However, one thing made her smile. She loved to serve food and work in the cafeteria. She gave a little—and we gave more. The cycle continued and eventually she was emotionally healed. Today she is married to a pastor and ministering to others.

How could working in a cafeteria change a person's life? God uses simple things to throw our analyzing abilities into the hopper! But that is the way He works. If we can understand Him, we really don't need Him because we would be able to figure out everything on our own.

## Let's get real...

- **How much time do you spend trying to analyze God's actions?**
- **When He speaks to you, do you immediately say, "I can't do that! It makes no sense."**
- **Do you need proof before you step out in obedience?**

God is no respecter of persons. He treats everyone alike, if we allow Him to do so. He is such a gentleman. He will not go against your will. He will speak if you are receptive to His voice.

What do the Scriptures have to say on this subject? The Bible is filled with promises. These promises are the inspired Word of God. Perhaps you will want to look up these Scriptures for yourself. Here are a few promises on the subject of listening from the New Living Translation:

1. Matthew 13:9: "Anyone with ears to hear should listen and understand."

2. Isaiah 59:1-2: "Listen! The LORD's arm is not too weak to save you, nor is his ear too deaf to hear you call. It's your sins that have cut you off from God. Because of your sins, he has turned away and will not listen anymore."

3. Isaiah 55:3: "Come to me with your ears wide open. Listen, and you will find life. I will make an everlasting covenant with you. I will give you all the unfailing love I promised to David."

4. Jeremiah 29:11-13: "For I know the plans I have for you," says the LORD. "They are plans for good and not for disaster, to give you a future and a hope. In those days when you pray, I will listen. If you look for me wholeheartedly, you will find me."

5. Psalm 91:15: "When they call on me, I will answer; I will be with them in trouble. I will rescue and honor them."

6. Mark 4:23-25: "Anyone with ears to hear should listen and understand." Then he added, "Pay close

> attention to what you hear. The closer you listen, the more understanding you will be given—and you will receive even more. To those who listen to my teaching, more understanding will be given. But for those who are not listening, even what little understanding they have will be taken away from them."

You might wonder how you can be sure it is God who speaks...

1. John 10:27 (NKJV): "My sheep hear My voice, and I know them, and they follow Me."

2. John 8:45 (NKJV): "But because I tell the truth, you do not believe Me."

3. In an interesting exchange between Pilate and Jesus before His crucifixion, this is what God's Word tells us in John 18:37 (NKJV): "Pilate therefore said to Him, 'Are You a king then?' Jesus answered, 'You say *rightly* that I am a king. For this cause I was born, and for this cause I have come into the world, that I should bear witness to the truth. Everyone who is of the truth hears My voice.'"

4. Revelation 3:20 (NLT): "Look! I stand at the door and knock. If you hear my voice and open the door, I will come in, and we will share a meal together as friends."

By this time perhaps you are wondering how God is going to speak to you personally—

- Will I hear a booming voice?
- Will He speak to me as I read His Word?
- Will He send an angel to me?
- Will He speak through prophecy? A dream? Or a vision?
- Will He speak through another person?
- Will I hear a "still, small voice" within me?

It can be one or maybe all of these ways.

As a seminary professor, Jack Deere believed that for centuries God spoke through prophecies, dreams, and visions, but when the Bible was complete—"Did God lose His voice?" During an intense study of God's Word, Jack discovered that God still speaks today apart from the Bible, but never in contradiction to the Bible.

From his book, *Surprised by the Voice of God*, (Zondervan, 1998) Jack writes:

> "No one found their way to the baby Jesus without direct revelation from the Holy Spirit. Zechariah knew what was about to happen because the angel Gabriel told him. Mary knew her womb would become His first home on earth because of Gabriel's announcement. Elizabeth had to be filled with the Holy Spirit in order to recognize Mary was carrying the Lord Jesus. Joseph had to be told in a dream or he would have divorced Mary. The shepherds found their way through an angelic announcement, and

the Magi were guided to Him by a star. Simeon and Anna were moved by the Holy Spirit to recognize Him and speak prophetically of His mission. The most striking absence at the birth of Jesus was that of the current reigning religious intelligentsia. *The Bible scholars of the day never made it to the manger.*"

Could it be that they heard from God but ignored Him? Maybe they simply could not believe that the King of Kings was coming into the world as a baby and would rest in a feed trough. For whatever reason, they missed the event. They missed eternal life.

*Father,*

*I pray that the reader of this book will hear Your voice.*

*Lord God, make the quiet times get better and better as You speak into each heart and life.*

*Father, don't let this reader believe that church attendance, a prayer here and there, Bible study, and Scripture reading are enough. Give them an insatiable hunger to spend more time with You, to learn to listen, to develop a loving and lasting relationship beyond their wildest imagination. Help them realize that when life makes no sense, You do!*

*Amen*

Chapter 3

# The Many Ways God Speaks to Us

God speaks to us in many ways. He speaks to us through:

- His Written Word
- The Holy Spirit
- The Still, Small Voice
- Visions and Dreams
- Prophecies
- Through Others
- Circumstances

Where can I get help in solving my problems? Who can I turn to in times in trouble and stress? How can I get an answer when there seems to be no solution? Are you searching, even now as you read this book, hoping you will find the answers to these questions? Hold fast...you are approaching your "Breakthrough!"

Several years ago, I met a poor, lonely divorced mother with three teenage daughters who was desperately searching for answers for her future. Kaye had few skills, not even a high school education. She was not receiving any kind of support from any source including her husband. She frantically read all kinds of secular self-help books—everything she could get her hands on—with no positive results. Things looked pretty grim.

One day someone introduced her to Jesus. It was that day the she discovered how God could be as big in her life as she would allow. She learned to hear His voice—sometimes through others, sometimes through His Word, and sometimes through His still, small voice.

It was not long before she acquired a job, a car, and the four bedroom home of which she had always dreamed. Kaye found answers to problems that seemed unsolvable by focusing on God, hearing His voice, and then being obedient.

## Let's get real...

- **Are you satisfied with your life? Are you where you thought you'd be by now?**
- **Can you identify wrong turns you've made and why you made them?**
- **Have you found your way back yet?**

Let's compare the situation you are now in to rowing a boat upstream against a mighty, rushing downstream current. You're exhausted and you seem to be regressing, or barely holding your own. It may be that you are divorced, raising your children by yourself, or maybe you are an unmarried single in the sunset years of your life. Perhaps you are married with a hurting teenager and there are so many problems for which you need answers. Don't be discouraged. Keep on searching. There IS an answer.

You've tried solving your own problems, charting your own course, doing your own thing, and still you find you are making no headway. Well-meaning people say it's tough to live the Christian life. Yet you can envision yourself cruising smoothly along, empowered by a supernatural force, with no resistance or fight, no struggle. You can imagine that easy and relaxing ride with God at the helm. Can you hear Him guiding you, sharing His solutions to your personal problems?

By now you are probably seriously considering giving God a chance to speak to you. It is okay if you belong to a church that never mentions such a thing as this. Even if you have never before considered this to be personally possible, go ahead and take a step out. This is scriptural! Can't you sense the Holy Spirit tugging on your heart strings? He wants you to find out more about Him and He wants to speak with you!

"Call to Me, and I will answer you, and show you great and mighty things, which you do not know" (Jeremiah 33:3 NKJV). How does He answer? Does His answer come in an audible voice? How can we expect to hear from Him? Many Christians think that God never speaks to them because no one ever told them He would.

How soon we forget our "born again" experience, when God first spoke to us through the power of His Holy Spirit and quickened us to receive Jesus. We responded to His "voice" by accepting Jesus as our Savior. This experience should lead us to seek other contacts with Him. If He spoke to us then, He can and will speak to us again and again.

## He Speaks Through His Word

First, and most importantly, God speaks to us through His Word. We need to have God's Word in our heart if we expect to hear from Him. God's written Word is full of answers to our questions and our problems. The reason most Christians do not hear from God is because they do not spend time reading the Bible. Hosea 4:6 (The Message) reminds us: "My people are ruined because they don't know what's right or true." Whose fault is this? God expects us to get into His Word. He holds us responsible for reading the Scriptures and knowing them.

The Holy Spirit can speak to us through the Word of God. John 16:13 (NKJV) says, "However, when He, the Spirit of truth, has come, He will guide you into all truth; for He will not speak on His own *authority*; but whatever He hears He will speak; and He will tell you things to come." Isn't it exciting to know that He will even tell us things to come? We need not be in ignorance, nor in darkness concerning anything, for He will tell us, through His Word.

We need to have His Word in our heart, for He speaks to us from the inside out, not from the outside in. By faith, we must act in harmony with His Word. His answer always lines up with His Word. Some Christians don't spend enough time in God's Word to know His voice. They think whatever comes into their minds is God speaking to them.

My family always prayed that my father would live to an old age with no serious illness. On Valentine's Day, at 3:00 in the morning, I was awakened by a phone call telling me my eighty-two-year-old father had just gone on to be with the Lord. It was a shock to be awakened with that unexpected news, but God uses His Word to restore and comfort us. My Bible fell open to Psalm 118:24 (NKJV): "This *is* the day *which* the LORD has made; We will rejoice and be glad in it."

This comforting word from my heavenly Father brought back many happy memories, as this was a verse my earthly father quoted every morning! And, by the way, he died with no serious illness. He breathed out here and breathed in to heaven.

We can be so familiar and filled with the touching life of Jesus Christ that we can instantly determine whether or not a thought is from Him.

## Let's get real...

- **Do you recognize the voice of a close friend when you hear it?**
- **Do you know it every time you hear it?**
- **Are you spending more time with your earthly best friend or your heavenly best Friend?**

Your spirit should recognize God's voice once you truly know Him through His Word. The Spirit of God will never guide you in opposition to the written Word of God. That's why it is so important to be familiar with what the Word really says. If not, you can easily be deceived. Be obedient in reading the written Word and you will become spiritually mature. Learn how to tune your inward ear to hear the Spirit of God. As you read God's Word you become mature in this, and you can **expect** to hear from Him.

I believe God wants us to sharpen our spiritual ears as we spend time in His Word. How does staying in His Word sharpen our ears? Joshua 1:8 (NKJV) says, "This Book of the Law shall not depart from your mouth, but you shall meditate in it day and night, that you may observe to do according to all that is written in it. For then you will make your way prosperous, and then you will have good success." We become familiar with God's voice because we get to know Him as we meditate upon His Word.

## He Speaks Through the Holy Spirit

Another way God speaks to us is through His Holy Spirit. Jesus said, "If anyone loves Me, he will keep My word; and My Father will love him, and We will come to him and make Our home with him" (John 14:23 NKJV). If God is dwelling in our hearts He communicates with us through our spirit. The prerequisite to hearing from God is that we be "born again" as a true Christian for we must have the Spirit of God abiding in our spirit before we can hear from Him.

We who are the sons and daughters of God can expect to be led by the Spirit of God. Romans 8:14 (NLT) says, "For all who are led by the Spirit of God are children of God." Therefore, we as Christians, can expect God's guidance at all times, for we are His children and we have His

Spirit. Nowhere in the Bible are we told that God will guide us by our physical bodies, or by our minds. God is a Spirit and He will guide us through our spirit, if we allow Him. "The Spirit Himself bears witness with our spirit that we are children of God" (Romans 8:16 NKJV).

Jesus said His sheep know His voice, and a stranger's voice they will not follow. John 10:27 (NKJV) says, "My sheep hear My voice, and I know them, and they follow Me." According to Romans 8:14, hearing the voice of the Spirit is a privilege that belongs to every believer.

There are people who are so busy looking for the spectacular that they fail to see the supernatural which is right there before them. For example, one day I was impressed to call someone with whom I did not ordinarily communicate. She answered the phone and said, "I am so glad you called. I've been sick and need a prescription filled and some groceries. Thank God. He heard my prayer and sent you to help me."

There was no big ticker-tape parade. My name did not go up in lights and this event did not even make the news. However, I knew that I had made a difference in her life. Why? Because I heard that still, small voice of the Lord that urged me to call her...*and I obeyed.*

Remember the Old Testament story of Gideon and his fleece? Even after he had heard from the angel of the Lord, he still wanted further proof that he had heard God's voice. Gideon had no prophet to assist him. Gideon was not baptized in the Holy Spirit. God graciously relieved his human doubts, acting upon the fleece as Gideon requested. How fortunate we are that Jesus can baptize us with His

Holy Spirit today to help us, to teach, lead, and guide us in every area of our lives.

Will you make a commitment today to give your attention to the Holy Spirit? Determine to yield to His voice and not the voices of the world, the flesh, or the devil.

## He Speaks Through the Inner Witness (That Still, Small Voice)

The inner witness, through the Holy Spirit operating in our minds, causes us to think the thoughts of Jesus. We find in 1 Corinthians 2:16 (The Message) the answer to Isaiah's question:

> 'Is there anyone around who knows God's Spirit, anyone who knows what he is doing?'...Christ knows, and we have Christ's Spirit.

That would include us!

More good news can be found in 1 Corinthians 1:30 (The Message):

> Everything that we have—right thinking and right living, a clean slate and a fresh start—comes from God by way of Jesus Christ.

Psalm 32:8 (NKJV) provides a promise that says, "I will instruct you and teach you in the way you should go; I will guide you with My eye."

The inner witness acts as a stop or go sign, a red or green traffic light inside of us. In John 16:13 (NKJV) we learn about truth. "However, when He, the Spirit of truth, has come, He will guide you into all truth; for He will not speak on His own *authority,* but whatever He hears He will speak; and He will tell you things to come." We need not put out a fleece as Gideon did, neither do we need to see "handwriting on the wall" (Daniel 5). When we are in the Word, and we have the Spirit of God dwelling in us, we will know the way we should go. God leads us by that inner witness as we listen to His leading. He is there, ready to speak to us.

A girl in the House of Hope program had reached a plateau in her healing and growth in the Lord. Later I learned that she had been too ashamed to confess something she felt was a horrible series of events in her past. The Holy Spirit impressed upon me through a word of knowledge that this girl had been taken advantage of and sexually molested by her brother when she was a little girl.

One night while we were talking I shared this with her. Not only did this strengthen her faith knowing that God had spoken to me, but she was astonished that He cared so much about her that He would speak to me about this to help rid her of this dark area of hurt and help bring healing. After this breakthrough she began growing spiritually at a rapid pace.

We must have our spiritual dial tuned in to God's channel at all times. There have been many times when the Lord has spoken to me and I have paid no attention (as unbelievable as that sounds). Just recently my niece who attends a local university spent the night with me before flying out the next morning. Before we left for the airport, she remembered that she had left an article of clothing that she needed to take with her in her apartment. Immediately the Lord spoke to me in that still, small voice and told me to let her take my car, because her own car would break down. I ignored the prompting. In less than an hour she called to ask if someone could pick her up because her car had broken down! How many times could tragedies be prevented if only we would listen?

## Let's get real...

- **Have you ever ignored the nudges of the Holy Spirit?**
- **Does God ever say, "I told you so?"**
- **How do you respond when you realize that you've been disobedient?**

There is always a way back and it starts with a repentant and humble heart.

Recently I was sitting in church beside a young couple when I had a strong urge to give them twenty dollars for no obvious reason. In my mind I thought: "Should I?" For many reasons some people are not good receivers. I wondered if it would offend them if I was obedient to that voice within me and gave them the money. This is the story the wife related to me several hours later when she excitedly called me on the telephone:

> Recently my husband and I were discussing our food budget. My sister was coming to visit us for nine days. After carefully planning our meals for nine days I could see that the food would cost more

than what was in our limited budget. It was wishful thinking to believe we could afford a $48.00 grocery bill since our finances were at very low ebb. My husband had recently changed jobs.

I said to my husband: "We always have paid our tithes first and then our bills." My husband said he couldn't do that because we already had a check that bounced. My heart skipped at the thought of not tithing, so I cut corners even more. And now the food list amounted to approximately $32.00, which both pleased and relieved my husband. I asked if he could now pay our tithe the next day at church and he said yes.

Earlier my husband had been talking to his parents on the telephone. His father was having severe back problems, to the extent that surgery seemed inevitable. My husband shared with his dad that the Lord would heal him.

The next morning we went to church. I could not see what my husband placed in the offering envelope. As we were leaving church Sara placed a $20.00 bill in my hand saying, "The Lord told me to give this to you." I was shocked! How did she know that we were having financial problems? I gave the money to my husband and he also was shocked because this exactly replaced our entire tithe (one tenth of our earnings) that he had just placed in the offering!

It is important to note that my husband told me that the night before he made the decision not to tithe, but after thinking about his conversation with his father, he changed his mind. He had decided that if he had enough faith to tell his dad that our Lord could heal his back, then he could trust Him with our finances too.

Looking back, I saw that God allowed us to make the decision to trust Him and to be obedient, even in times which seemed to us a financial crisis. I made the decision to submit to my husband by cutting down the grocery list. My husband witnessed the healing love of God to his father, then he made a decision to be obedient to God's Word concerning tithing. We knew in our spirits that the money Sara gave us was God's way of saying, "You were obedient, I knew you couldn't afford it, but I wanted you to trust me."

After listening to her story I knew that the thought to give them the $20.00 was not from my mind, but from that "still, small voice" from within. What a blessing to hear from God!

Did you ever lose something and, after searching for hours and maybe even days, you finally, in desperation, sat down and said: "Oh, Lord where could that thing be?" Suddenly He drops the answer into your inner spirit. That thought is His "still, small voice." Upon hearing that still, small voice you immediately go and look, and there it is! If only we had called on the Lord first, think of all the time we would have saved. How pleased He is when we seek Him first.

Some time ago a friend gave me a beautiful set of cloisonné beads which I just loved. One day my lovely beads disappeared. I hunted high and low, under cushions, crawled around looking under furniture, desperately searching for my lost treasure. It was then the Lord spoke to me and said, "If you will search for Me with all your heart…as you search for that which is lost…I will reveal Myself to you." Deuteronomy 4:29 (NLT) says, "But from there you will search again for the Lord your God. And if you search for him with all your heart and soul, you will find him."

Again, in Proverbs 2:4-6 (NKJV) we are told, "If you seek her as silver, and search for her as *for* hidden treasures; then you will understand the fear of the LORD, and find the knowledge of God. For the LORD gives wisdom; from His mouth *come* knowledge and understanding."

By the way, after praying I did find my beads. I had pulled my sweater over my head and they were in the sweater.

## He Speaks Through Prophecies

Occasionally God speaks to us through prophecies. When the gifts of the Holy Spirit are in operation in a church, God sometimes guides through prophetic ministries, which are judged. We find instructions in 1 Corinthians 14:29 (NKJV) which reads, "Let two or three prophets speak, and let the others judge." It is important to know the character of the individuals who are prophesying. There should also be other evidence to confirm the prophecy, before acting on whatever the prophet(s) relate. 1 Thessalonians 5:20-21 (NKJV) exhorts us to, "Do not despise prophecies. Test all things; hold fast what is good." Usually the prophecy we receive can be confirmation to reassure us of something that God has already told us.

At a recent weekend seminar for fellowship group leaders, God spoke specifically to me through Marilyn Hickey with the following scripture from Psalm 50:15. Marilyn pointed directly and said she had a rhema word from the Lord for me concerning a situation. The King James reads, "And call upon Me in the day of trouble and I will deliver thee and thou shalt glorify Me" (KJV). She went further to say, "You have already called on Him and there is only a little dark edge left that is about to break loose—about to break through—and this will happen to bring glory to His name." There is evidence of these words of knowledge and wisdom already bearing fruit as a situation unfolded.

## He Speaks Through Visions and Dreams

God sometimes speaks to us through dreams and visions. When He speaks to us in this way it should be supported by other confirmations, and not taken alone as being the sole interpretation of His speaking to us. The Spirit-filled believer may experience dreams and visions, as a means of God speaking.

> And it shall come to pass afterward that I will pour out My Spirit on all flesh; your sons and your daughters shall prophesy, your old men shall dream dreams, your young men shall see visions... (Joel 2:28 NKJV ).

> For God speaks again and again, though people do not recognize it. He speaks in dreams, in visions of the night, when deep sleep falls on people as they lie

in their beds. He whispers in their ears and terrifies them with warnings (Job 33:14-16 NLT).

Several years ago I was on my knees preparing for communion in the Episcopal Church. What seemed to be only seconds turned into approximately fifteen-minutes. I was nudged by the usher that it was my time to receive communion. What had actually happened I shall never forget: God had spoken to me through a vision and the extent and depth I cannot describe. It should be pointed out, however, that one important part of the vision was that the Lord spoke and said I would be teaching that Jesus Christ is alive today and that I would be leading people.

Only two weeks later, my priest called me into his office and said he felt God was telling him to ask me to teach 'Life in the Spirit" (a seminar on the Spirit-led living). I was not surprised because it had been confirmed through the vision I had received earlier. It was a confidence builder and great spiritual boost to be able to do this on God's power and not my own.

I received another confirmation of what the Lord had told me when two elderly sisters (ages seventy-five and seventy-eight) came up during my Sunday morning class. Kathryn, the older asked me to pray for her sister, Martha. She had not been able to bend her painful knee for the past several years. The doctor had told her she never would be able to have full use of her knee again.

That morning Martha was healed and danced all over the front of the church. Because the Lord had already told me I would be used in healing her, it gave me confidence to continue to pray for others as well as to keep going with the seminars.

Once I was praying for a teenage girl who was having many problems stemming from fears. As I was praying the Lord gave me a picture in my mind (a vision) of a little girl (approximately three years old) in a blue short-sleeved dress, sitting on the sidewalk crying. As we prayed, the Lord spoke to me and said: "It was at this time that fear came in." After we finished praying she said, "You know, as you were praying, I saw myself as a little girl in a blue short-sleeved dress sitting on the sidewalk crying."

I asked her if she remembered any traumatic experience about that time in her life. She couldn't remember, but when her dad came to pick her up he had the answer. He related a story of when she was three years old as she was playing on the sidewalk she was caught between a boy on his bicycle and a dog on his chain. The dog lunged at her and ripped open a pie-shaped wound in her check which exposed her bottom teeth. She was alone at the time of this terrifying experience and rushed to the hospital. Uncovering that fear helped her receive her healing that day!

Praise the Lord! He uses whatever way He chooses to speak to us as we are "tuned in" to hear from Him.

## Let's get real...

- **Has God ever revealed something about someone else and wanted you to share it with them?**

- **Were you obedient or did you chicken out because it was too weird for you—and for the other person?**
- **Why do you think God plants those visions in your heart?**
- **Are you totally convinced that they are from the Lord?**

What will it take to convince you? The more time you spend with Him, the more He will speak to you. Sometimes His words are out of the ordinary—especially when it comes to others. But rest assured, if you are in sync with Him, you will be able to step out and feel no fear or anxiety as you speak into the lives of others.

## He Speaks Through Other People

One morning, as I was brushing my hair, preparing to go to the airport to pick up a Ladies Aglow speaker, the Lord spoke to me in that inner voice and said, 'I want you to give Faith your gold cross." (Faith was the name of the speaker!) Surely God didn't mean my new gold cross which was just recently given to me. I promptly tried to put out of my mind the idea of giving away the cross. "Not this gold one," I thought. "Surely God wouldn't want me to give up this treasure that had just been given to me." When I greeted Faith at the airport, she was wearing a plain gold chain. During the drive home, she revealed that the Lord had told her that someone was going to give her a gold cross.

I shared with her that the Lord had told me to give her the cross. I didn't want to give it up, but in obedience to

God, I did. God is so good...about two weeks after this incident someone gave me another cross identical to the one I had given away! You experience great spiritual growth when God confirms His Word through another person.

Over a period of five years I have received prophecies from three reliable ministries cautioning me that there would be people who would try to get involved in the House of Hope ministry for selfish reasons. This first one was as follows: "There are those would like to capitalize on what you have and do. Don't sell out to another system. Allow Me to do it through you. I will bring in those to sustain, support, provide, guide, and direct."

The second minister prophesied a year later, "I must caution you: Beware of those who would try to influence you. Do not listen to man. I will speak to you by the soft whisper of my Holy Spirit. Again I say do not listen to men who are out for selfish gain." I actually ignored the first prophecy. When the second one was given to me I began to take notice for I was already aware of several times when people had tried to get involved for selfish gain.

One of the nation's largest ministries sent someone to me to help with fund development. Not long after, that lady had been recommended to help out with a larger project from the same ministry. In my trusting naivety, I thought that we were getting blessed. What I did not know was that this was a set up for their personal gain. Through other people, the Holy Spirit revealed that these two married people were having an affair and had made this arrangement under the guise of helping us. Needless to say, both were terminated on the spot. If God had not intervened, the situation could have proven costly in many ways. Thank God for His revelation!

I began to become alert and vigilant. By the time the third prophecy was given I had become keenly aware and more protective of House of Hope. I realized that God had been trying to get my attention over the years so I would listen to Him and not man. These prophecies have been confirmed over and over.

God sometimes speaks to us through others as we listen for His voice. There is a principle of kingdom authority and we should never make a major decision for our lives until we first sit down with a man or woman of God, and together seek His leading.

We must submit to those who have authority over us. Hebrews 13:17 (NKJV) instructs us, "Obey those who rule over you, and be submissive, for they watch out for your souls, as those who must give account. Let them do so with joy and not with grief, for that would be unprofitable for you."

Watch out for others' messages for you. God doesn't usually go through a third party when He has a message for you. He will come directly to you if you are in the Word, your eyes are on Jesus, and if you are in the habit of listening to the Lord. He probably would not bypass you and tell someone else. He has many messages for you—points concerning your discipline and growth. It is not likely He would relay to someone else the message He has for you (except for confirmation). If you are not ready to hear it from the Lord directly, you probably are not ready to hear it from someone else.

An evangelist came to me once saying that the Lord had impressed upon him the fact that I was to accompany Him to Africa. I felt flattered, and told him I would pray about it, yet I knew in my spirit (that inner witness) that I was not meant to go. How tragic if I had listened to a person instead of to God. We need to get out of the flesh and be led by the Holy Spirit if we are to receive true guidance from God.

## Let's get real...

- **Have you ever asked someone else to give you a Word from God?**
- **Have you ever been in a service where everyone was receiving a Word from God *except* you?**
- **Why do you feel the need to receive a Word from someone else?**

God does have a word for you. In fact, He has a whole Bible filled with words for you. Have you heard someone say: "Pray and see what God tells you about me?" We should remind them that God wants to speak to them personally. He doesn't need an interpreter to act as His go-between. I know I keep coming back to this scripture, but you need to get this deep into your spirit. Jeremiah 33:3 (NKJV) says, "Call to Me, and I will answer you, and show you great and mighty things, which you do not know." That's a promise.

Sometimes God's voice is revealed through the experiences of life. Our victories, our trials, our goof-ups are all great teachers. Oswald Chambers once said, "If we refuse to listen to Him, He will move in as an engineer—engineering the circumstances of our life to get our full attention."

## He Speaks Through Circumstances

God speaks through circumstances. We must try to judge and discern what He is trying to say through the events in our lives. We should always be alert to what God is trying to say to us in every circumstance in our life. Is God trying to speak to you through the circumstances in your life? We must be willing to obey once we are convinced we have heard from God. He sees the intent of our hearts and He will not speak if He knows we will not listen!

Sometimes God gets our attention through successes, disappointments, and even through failures because we haven't listened. John Wimber once prayed, "Well, Father, You know and I know I can't do anything—so show me what You are doing and draw me into that."

Each one of us is unique and special to God. We all can hear from Him. We all will hear from Him in the way that He knows is right for us. He speaks in different ways because His children are so different. He will speak to you today if you will seek Him and listen.

Your answers will come:

- through God's written Word
- through the Holy Spirit
- through the inner witness, that still, small voice
- through a dream or vision
- through prophecy

- through other people
- through circumstances.

If only you will be obedient and sincerely desire to hear from Him.

## Chapter 4

# Obedience

"But you, when you pray, go into your room, and when you have shut your door, pray to your Father who *is* in the secret *place;* and your Father who sees in secret will reward you openly." —Matthew 6:6 (NKJV)

"Ask, and it will be given to you; seek, and you will find; knock, and it will be opened to you. For everyone who asks receives, and he who seeks finds, and to him who knocks it will be opened." —Matthew 7:7-8 (NKJV)

### Listening to Become Disciplined Disciples

We need to come to God with a child-like attitude or the attitude of Samuel. "Then God came and stood before him exactly as before, calling out, "Samuel! Samuel!" Samuel answered, "Speak. I'm your servant, ready to listen" (1 Samuel 3:10 The Message).

We should devote quality time daily in just being quiet and listening to Him. We all seem to have a tendency to allow our busy schedule and the cares of the world to shut God out. We really need to spend quality time each day, not just at times when we can squeeze in a few minutes.

We must realize just how important our "divine appointments" really are. If we were to make an appointment with our doctor, hairdresser, or breakfast with friends, we would make sure we keep that appointment—*and arrive on time.*

How much more important our appointment is with the Creator of the Universe, our Savior and our Lord! We prove how little we really love Him when we choose to listen to television rather than to Him. We prefer to listen to Christian messages on tapes and hear personal testimonies, rather than taking that time to be alone with God to allow Him to speak directly to us. Why is that? Could it be that we are afraid of what we might hear Him say? It is easier not to allow Him to speak to us at all rather than for Him to speak to us and ignore what He says.

When God speaks to us we have the choice of whether to listen to Him or willfully and deliberately ignore Him and live with the guilt of knowing we have chosen to disobey Him. Adam and Eve heard His voice, "So he said, 'I heard Your voice in the garden, and I was afraid because I was naked; and I hid myself'" (Genesis 3:10 NKJV). It was guilt and shame that made them fear and hide from His voice. It wasn't the nakedness of their bodies that disturbed them the most, it was that God could see into their hearts and He knew them inside and out.

# Let's get real...

- **Have you ever been embarrassed knowing that God saw you or heard you doing something that was ungodly?**
- **Can you remember a time when you got that uncomfortable feeling in the pit of your stomach and ignored it anyway? What were the results? What did you learn?**
- **How does God want you to respond when you have been "found out?"**

The Bible reminds us that obedience is far better than sacrifice. There are two prerequisites for listening to our Lord:

- The desire to hear what Jesus Christ is saying.
- The obedient daily sacrifice of our time.

After we listen, we need to be obedient and do what He tells us to do. As I was listening to the Lord one day this is what I heard:

> "There is something about which I should discipline you: Take My yoke upon you. Don't try to run ahead of Me. There are important things you will miss if you go too fast. It's like traveling across the country. There are many beautiful joys and situations you never experience when you fly, there are many lovely views that you cannot appreciate when you go by jet."

The Lord was saying: "Wait upon Me. Sara, listen to Me and take My yoke upon you" (from Matthew 11:29). The yoke is a frame within which we are joined to Jesus, coupled with the Holy Spirit to serve God. Every morning, upon arising, I must allow myself to be yoked and harnessed with Jesus, in order for the Holy Spirit to operate in my life. Jesus must be given authority. I must commit myself to His direction and listen to what He wants to say to me.

In Jeremiah 6:16 (NKJV), the Lord reminds us to "Stand in the ways and see, and ask for the old paths, where the good way *is,* and walk in it; then you will find rest for your souls. But they said, 'We will not walk *in it.*'" We are to be yoked with our Lord Jesus. Until we are united with Him, our souls will never be at rest. Every action we take, every move we make, yokes us either with Jesus, or with Satan. We cannot bear the burden and pressure that Satan would attempt to place upon us. With Jesus we can stand firm, for He has given us the whole armor of God (Ephesians 6:10-20) to protect us.

We have authority through Him. If we are yoked with Jesus and have the Holy Spirit dwelling in us, then the fruit of the Spirit is evident in our lives (Galatians 5:22):

- Love
- Joy
- Peace
- Longsuffering
- Kindness
- Goodness
- Faithfulness
- Gentleness
- Self-control

Satan would prefer to keep us under bondages of:

- Sin
- Fear
- Darkness
- Perversion

- Doubt
- Unbelief
- Anxiety
- Deception
- Rejection
- Hate
- Anger
- Rebellion
- And all other works of darkness
- Lust
- Unhappiness
- Occult Involvement
- Evil
- Witchcraft
- Rock Music
- Drugs/alcohol
- Cigarettes

Satan has come to:

- Kill
- Steal
- Destroy

The yoke of Jesus is:

- Light
- Truth
- Life

Satan's yoke is heavy with:

- Depression
- Desperation
- Death

A friend of mine shared with me a chart (on page 58) that we can check ourselves for one week to find out if we have the fruits of the Spirit or if we are in the flesh. If you seriously consider this, and ask God what He is saying, it will change your life!

## A Seven Day Heart Inspection

For each day and each fruit, place a G if you are listening to God; a F if listening to the flesh.

| Fruits of the Spirit | S 1 | M 2 | T 3 | W 4 | Th 5 | F 6 | S 7 | Fruits of the Flesh |
|---|---|---|---|---|---|---|---|---|
| Love—Does not seek her own way, is not selfish or self-centered | | | | | | | | Selfish, self-centered full of lust |
| Joy—Love doesn't rejoice in iniquity but rather rejoices in truth | | | | | | | | Anger, self pity, negative |
| Peace—Love is not easily provoked, but is serene and stable | | | | | | | | Worried, fearful, touchy, gluttonous |
| Patience—Love suffers long, perseveres, and is patient | | | | | | | | Quick tempered, irritable, fretful |
| Kindness—Love is merciful, thoughtful and concerned, it envies not. | | | | | | | | Unmerciful, envious, harsh-critical |
| Goodness— Love is great, gracious, and generous, it is kind and good | | | | | | | | Rough-rude, resentful, selfish |
| Faithfulness—Love thinks no evil but has faith in God and others | | | | | | | | Lying-deceitful, gossipy, won't trust God |
| Meekness— Love is humble and gentle, doesn't flaunt itself | | | | | | | | Proud-boastful, lacking in prayer, vain and conceited |
| Self-Control— Love is disciplined and controlled, doesn't behave unbecomingly | | | | | | | | Undisciplined, procrastinates, lustful |

How do we become yoked with Jesus Christ? We must learn to listen. Before we can learn to listen and grow, we must become obedient. We must be willing to listen and be chastened and reproved by Him in order to improve. We are told in the Bible that God teaches (or chastens) those whom He loves in order to make them more perfect, more obedient.

Samuel speaks to Saul in the book of 1 Samuel 15:22 (Living Bible): "Obedience is far better than sacrifice. He is much more interested in your listening to Him than in your offering the fat of rams to Him. For rebellion is as bad as the sin of witchcraft, and stubbornness is as bad as worshipping idols."

Fasting is another way we can get God's attention. Fasting is not intended as a means of twisting God's arm. As we look at Joel 1:14 we find an example of a proclaimed fast. The purpose is to bring us into one accord as we are obedient in pray and fasting to hear God's voice, and to find out what we can do about a situation.

In 2 Chronicles 20 the Ammonites came against Jehoshaphat to battle. Jehoshaphat was afraid. He set himself to seek the Lord and proclaim a fast. He sought the Lord concerning the protection of Judah. Then the spirit of the Lord spoke to them and said, "Do not be afraid...the battle *is* not yours, but God's" (2 Chronicles 20:15 NKJV).

The Holy Spirit then spoke to them and told them ...

- What to say
- How to say it, and
- When to say it

They followed God's instructions and, honoring their obedience in listening, God made them victorious. In fact, God made them more than victorious. The result was that their enemies destroyed themselves and Jehoshaphat's army went in and could not carry away all the riches left by the enemy...it took three days to collect it all!

An example of how God spoke to the people in the New Testament concerning fasting is told in Acts 13:2 (NKJV). At the church of Antioch, certain prophets and teachers had gathered together to pray and fast and minister to the Lord. There they were, just a group of men sitting around praying and fasting. "As they ministered to the Lord and fasted, the Holy Spirit said, 'Now separate to Me Barnabas and Saul for the work to which I have called them.'" Paul and Barnabas were just prophets and teachers before the Holy Spirit spoke—now they were anointed to be apostles. What the Holy Spirit said changed the world, and is still changing us. In fact, two-thirds of the New Testament came into existence because of what Paul experienced as a result of listening.

Many times, as I listen to the Lord, He gives me special people for whom He wants me to pray (not only to pray, but to follow the instructions for those people whatever they may be). On one occasion as I listened, the Lord told me to pray for someone named Frances. I tried to think of anyone I might know with the name of Frances, but to no avail. However, I wrote the name at the top of my prayer list and continued to pray for Frances. After several days of praying I was visiting my parents in North Carolina when a couple, whom I had never met, came by to visit. You guessed it, the wife's name was Frances! With tears in her eyes, she said: "Honey, thank you, I was in the hospital two days ago, the doctors said I had cancer. I called Oral Roberts University Prayer Tower for prayers. They took me in for x-rays before operating, and the growth had disappeared! Thank you for your prayers."

She then asked me to pray for a knot on her hand because there was a growth about the size of a walnut on top of her hand and it had been there for years. I laid hands on it and prayed. The next day my mother and I were at the local gas station when who should drive up but the same couple. The husband jumped out of his car excitedly, rushed over to our car and said: "Praise God, the knot on Frances' hand has totally disappeared. She is healed!" To God be the glory.

We must ever remind ourselves that listening, without acting in obedience to what we have heard, is displeasing to God. We are to be doers of His Word, as well as hearers. Hear what our Lord had to say to Cain:

> The LORD said to Cain: "What's wrong with you? Why do you have such an angry look on your face? If you had done the right thing, you would be smiling. But you did the wrong thing, and now sin is waiting to attack you like a lion. Sin wants to destroy you, but don't let it!'" (Genesis 4:6-7, CEV).

Our Lord reminds us that if we will listen to Him, we will become conquerors with Him. "Yet in all these things we are more than conquerors through Him who loved us" (Romans 8:37 NKJV).

You don't have to be on your knees, alone in quiet meditation, to hear from the Lord. One day as I was driving along to work praying, I heard "that still, small voice" within me say, "Pray for your brother in North Carolina." I obeyed that voice with a prayer of protection for my brother. That night I received a telephone call from my mother informing me that my brother had been involved in an automobile accident that morning. A careless driver had totally demolished his car...my brother walked away from the accident with only a broken fingernail! What if I hadn't known how to listen? What if I had not heeded and prayed for him? Praise God for the chance to be tuned in.

Chapter 5

# Checkpoints

A pilot checks his instruments as he prepares for take-off. Certain readings be must taken to be sure there are no problem areas which would prevent his safe ascent. So it is with us, as we prepare to hear from God. There are certain areas that we must check out if our prayers are to get through to Him.

## Before Hearing From God

You must get rid of excess baggage including...

- Unconfessed Sin
- Unforgiveness
- Wavering Faith
- Impure Thoughts
- Occult Involvement
- Bondages
- Anything that brings chaos and spiritual darkness into your life

Before we seek to hear from God, let's look at several areas in our lives which we will need to check so there will be:

- No blockage
- No interference
- No static on the line that would make for a bad connection.

We need to check these things:

- Is there a corner in our life which we have not truly surrendered to God?
- Have we been obedient?
- Have we confessed and renounced all known sin in our life?
- Have we totally forgiven everyone?
- Have we prayed in the name of Jesus?
- Have we asked according to God's will?
- Do we, by faith, expect an answer?
- Have we broken all bondages?

This list probably looks overpowering, but we know we can't do any of these by ourselves. We must be willing to surrender and to have God step in. God will take over as He knows the attitude of our hearts.

> "Search me, O God, and know my heart; try me, and know my anxieties; and see if *there is any* wicked way in me, and lead me in the way everlasting."
> —Psalms 139:23-24 (NKJV)

"In your relationships with one another, have the same attitude of mind Christ Jesus had." —Philippians 2:5 (TNIV)

"Nothing in life is as important as attitude. The remarkable thing is we have a choice every day regarding the attitude we will embrace. We cannot change our past...the only thing we can do is play on the one string we have, and that is our attitude... I am convinced that life is ten percent what happens to me and ninety percent how I react to it. And so it is with you...we are in charge of our attitudes."

—Chuck Swindoll

It is impossible to hide what is in the heart. "Counsel in the heart of man *is like* deep water, but a man of understanding will draw it out." —Proverbs 20:5 (NJKV)

Often we don't have to work very hard at bringing up our own conscious mind. What our heart contains will be displayed to the world by the words that come out of our mouths (Luke 6:45).

# Let's get real...

- **What is your attitude about life?**
- **What is the first thing you think of when you wake up each morning?**
- **How do you spend your last waking moments before you drift off to sleep?**
- **Do you want to know the truth?**

> "If ye continue [abide] in my word, then are ye my disciples indeed; and ye shall know the truth, and the truth shall make you free." —John 8:31-32 (KJV)

I know that the truth can free you, but few really want to know the truth in that kind of depth.

Let's look more closely at each of the above areas separately. Let's relate each area to God's Word: Is there any corner of our lives which we have not surrendered completely to God? Is there any area in which you have not truly been obedient? "And whatever we ask we receive from Him, because we keep His commandments and do those things that are pleasing in His sight" (1 John 3:22 NKJV).

Have you confessed and renounced all known sin in your life? This is a must. "If we confess our sins, He is faithful and just to forgive us *our* sins and to cleanse us from all unrighteousness" (1 John 1:9 NKJV). This is just between God and us. 1 John 3:21-22 (NKJV) says, "Beloved, if our heart does not condemn us, we have confidence toward God. And whatever we ask we receive from Him, because we keep His commandments and do those things that are pleasing in His sight."

David said in Psalm 66:18 (NKJV): "If I regard iniquity in my heart, the Lord will not hear." Let's check to see if we are ignoring areas of disobedience. We need to stop lying to ourselves that we don't really have dark areas that need to be exposed to the sunlight of God's forgiving love. Let's get rid of any barrier that might prevent God from hearing us when we call on Him.

For over a year I had been trying to stop smoking. At the same time God was trying to get my attention concerning the barriers of ego and pride. I had mixed emotions. I wanted to stop, yet I really enjoyed smoking. I was so hooked on cigarettes that I thought I couldn't enjoy going to the beach or even talking with friends unless I could smoke.

Finally I asked someone to pray for me to stop, and because she prayed I assumed it would be easy for me to stop. Because I refused to carry cigarettes I thereby restrained myself, but it was only temporary. My belief was that it wouldn't matter if I smoked just one after each meal, but two days later I was back smoking worse than ever. Feelings of guilt swept over me. I felt like a phony, because I was teaching an adult Bible class every Sunday and I didn't want them to know that I smoked. To make matters worse, about a week later I was invited by the one who had prayed for me to give my "Victory Over Cigarette Smoking" testimony before a large number of people. My poor pride and ego were hurting! How I hated to have to tell her I had lost the battle.

She so understood and suggested I have more prayers. Again I sought out someone to pray with me. I temporarily stopped smoking with a struggle and again was overpowered by the urge to smoke, even though I really wanted to stop. I was smoking more cigarettes in one day than I had ever smoked before. Instead of improving I seemed to be going downhill rapidly. Worse yet, I was invited again by the same friend to travel to a nearby city to give "The Testimony" which I didn't have! And once again I had to swallow my pride and go through the embarrassment of admitting my newest failure. Then I really began seeking the Lord. I called on Him in desperation and cried, "Lord, I **do** want to stop, but I **can't**." He said, "I know **you** can't, but you will be delivered of smoking in December at the Frances and Charles Hunter meeting." You can't imagine the excitement of knowing that I knew that I knew.

A few weeks later the Hunters came to town. For the entire fifteen-mile drive I chain-smoked and they never tasted better. I finished the last cigarette that I would ever smoke as I arrived at the door of the meeting. I knew that just as God said, I would be delivered. I handed the few cigarettes that were left in the pack and my lighter to a friend. I didn't want to carry them inside.

As I walked to the front, Frances pointed to me and said, "You are going to stop smoking tonight." As I left the front of the auditorium the front row was filled with members of a Bible class I was teaching! As I walked by several look horrified as they pointed and said, "Oh, we didn't know you smoked!" Satan wanted to get in one more stab at my pride. The barriers of pride and ego finally began to crumble.

That has been over thirty years ago and I haven't had the least desire to smoke since that time. I often think that I should have sought God first. He had the real solution. He will answer us when we seek Him.

By paying close attention to attitude, your reaction, God can reveal the root of the sin that has you bound. It's like pulling weeds in a garden. Cut them off and you prune them. They have to come out by the root!

When my attitude stinks, He invites me to a position of abandonment. That means dropping everything in my hand and coming to Christ—kneeling to His authority and Lordship, and placing my head in His yoke. His yoke is light. Why? Nothing is as heavy as having yourself on your hands. Being in control is a heavy issue. His invitation is to come and drop the weight.

> If you want to identify the hidden strongholds in your life, you need only to survey the attitudes of your heart. Every area in your thinking that glistens with hope in God is an area liberated by Christ. But any system of thinking that has no hope is a stronghold that must be pulled down.
>
> —Francis Frangipane

## Let's get real...

- **Is there any unforgiveness in your life?**
- **Do you feel that someone else is to blame?**

Perhaps you are thinking, "You don't know how badly that person has treated me." Forgiveness is not based on feelings; true forgiveness is a matter of our will. It means that we are willing to be willing. It doesn't mean that we feel like it. Mark 11:25 (NKJV) says, "And whenever you stand praying, if you have anything against anyone, forgive him, that your Father in heaven may also forgive you your trespasses."

As we look within ourselves, do we remember to pray in the name of Jesus? Ephesians 2:18 explains that the only way we have access to the Father is through Jesus. In Colossians 3:17 (NKJV) says, "And *whatever* you do in word or deed, *do* all in the name of the Lord Jesus, giving thanks to God the Father through Him." John 14:14 (NKJV) says: "If you anything in my name, I will do *it*." Let's check our request and be certain we ask in Jesus' name.

## What Are You Expecting?

We need to ask ourselves if we are truly expecting God to answer when we seek Him? Do we really believe He is hearing us? Do we doubt that He will answer? "But let him ask in faith, with no doubting, for he who doubts is like a wave of the sea driven and tossed by the wind" (James 1:6 NKJV). Matthew 21:22 (NKJV) says, "And whatever things you ask in prayer, believing, you will receive."

We need to stop begging and begin believing that God is hearing us when we call...and ***expect*** an answer. Jesus never failed to get answers...it is after Him that we should pattern our prayer life.

The original location of House of Hope was on about an acre. There was a large building on the back of the adjoining property that would have made a perfect gymnasium. So we began praying for the property. We got in touch with the owner to try to buy the property. His price was far too high. We kept pleading in our prayers for God to work it out so we could get the property.

After a couple of years, we found the property could not be sold because the property had a lien on it. Then we prayed for the state to release it to us as a 5OC3 ministry. That did not work either.

We could not understand why our prayers were not being answered. Then one day, we found out that state was taking the entire block (including our property) to widen Interstate 4. God blessed us with a financial settlement and moved us to a beautiful peninsula—a ten acre campus.

God heard our payers the moment we asked but he had something better in mind for us in His time!

Sometimes the devil does try to whisper in our ear and what he has to say has negative consequences and condemnation. Satan tries to lure us. John 10:10 (NKJV) teaches us, "The thief does not come except to steal, and to kill, and to destroy. I have come that they may have life, and that they may have *it* more abundantly." When Satan tries to put thoughts in our minds we can ignore him, for we have victory over him in the name of Jesus. Jesus gave us authority over Satan. He told us in James 4:7 (The Message), "So let God work his will in you. Yell a loud no to the Devil and watch him scamper." We can bind Satan and command him, in the name of Jesus, to take his hands off of God's property and he has to go.

Let's look at what our Lord has to say about our authority over him: "Behold, I give you the authority to trample on serpents and scorpions, and over all the power of the enemy, and nothing shall by any means hurt you" (Luke 10:19 NKJV). What a promise!

After we are certain that Satan is bound, we can go on to the next checkpoint.

> For though we walk in the flesh, we do not war after the flesh: (for the weapons of our warfare *are* not carnal, but mighty through God to the pulling

> down of strong holds;) Casting down imaginations, and every high thing that exalteth itself against the knowledge of God, and bringing into captivity every thought to the obedience of Christ. —2 Corinthians 10:3-5 (KJV)

Let's check ourselves to be sure we have placed all of our thoughts under God's captivity. Before we prepare to hear from God, you must take an active role in getting your mind and heart in order.

## Let's get real...

- **Have you confessed and renounced your known and unknown sins?**
- **Have you forgiven those who have hurt and offended you?**
- **Have you forgiven yourself?**
- **Have you broken all bondages that have separated you from God?**
- **Are you approaching God through Jesus and asking according to God's perfect will?**
- **Do you really expect an answer?**

Binding Satan and placing our thoughts under God's captivity is serious business. We lean not to our own understanding (Proverbs 3:5) and know that we can trust God to speak to us. We need to select a time when we are not in a hurry to go somewhere or in a rush to do something. We need to be alone and be quiet as we meditate on God's Word. We then can worship Him and listen to what He has to say to us. Hearing from God must be our top priority.

If you have reviewed the preceding checkpoints and met the conditions, you are now ready to call upon Him and He will answer.

Chapter 6

# Breakthrough

> My people are destroyed for lack of knowledge. Because you have rejected knowledge, I also will reject you from being priest for Me; because you have forgotten the law of your God, I also will forget your children (Hosea 4:6 NKJV).

## Time Out to Tune In

What a tragic commentary on our disobedience, our indifference, and our lack of love for the Word of God. We are held responsible for the amount of light (knowledge) we possess. We can operate only on that level at which we find ourselves. Are we willing to shake off our spiritual lethargy, open our Bible and receive words of light from the One who is *The Light*?

We need to obey God, but how can we know how to obey Him unless we read His Word? We can pray that the Holy Spirit will bring understanding to us. His Word will tell us things about ourselves, which we have never known. Our minds will be illumined with new thoughts, His thoughts, through that "still, small voice" within us. We can meditate upon (and even write down) some of the things that He says to us. We will be simply amazed to find how our spiritual horizons expand as we see what a magnificent Teacher we have in our Lord.

I will never forget the first time I heard Virginia Lively, an Episcopal lay-woman, speak on "Listening to the Lord." A whole new dimension opened to me. What an impact this had on me! It was evident that Virginia had an experience which I had never known. I did not even know it was possible.

Suddenly, as I listened, I wanted to have that same intimate relationship with Jesus that this speaker enjoyed. My thought was, "She seems to be nearer to God than any Christian I have ever known." I wanted that relationship and I wondered if this "listening relationship" could be why she had such a clear line of communication to heaven.

I decided to try it and it was at this point my life turned around. As I began to consider this more carefully, I came to understand that her "clear line to heaven" was the result of a sacrifice on her part, she had regularly set aside time for listening to God and reading His Word. It was a "breakthrough" for me when I realized that anyone could have that same beautiful relationship, if they were willing to pay the price.

If God wants His will to be done on this earth as it is in heaven—and He does—we need to start listening to Him and getting to know Him better.

I made the decision to get up an hour earlier each day and start my day with prayer, Bible reading, and listening to

His voice. It changed my life! However, I must tell you that it hasn't always been easy. There have been many distractions. The telephone would ring. Something would come up and remind me of a rapidly approaching appointment. There were emergencies with those rebellious teenagers. There was some unexpected meeting I needed to prepare for...quickly. A neighbor knocked on the door.

Yes, during those early times, I felt frustrated and lost my focus and often lost my cool. But through those distractions, here is what I learned to do:

1. Keep a notepad by your side.
2. Do not answer the telephone. Turn off your phone, your cell phone, and your pager.
3. Put out a do-not-disturb sign.
4. In your mind, make this the most special meeting of the day.
5. If you find there are too many distractions during the day, change your appointment time with God. He wants your undivided attention and He is available 24/7!

Because I could now see Him in a new and powerful way, I began to look at myself differently, longing to become more like Him. What spiritual blessings followed as I started this deeper walk with our Lord!

In the morning I usually write down what God says to me. After a busy day, as I relax before going to bed, I reread His words, and I am sometimes amazed at what I read, conscious of the fact that I could not have expressed myself in such a beautiful manner. The words I read had to be His words.

Most of the thoughts that He brings to mind are thoughts which I have never consciously entertained. (I now have several volumes filled with His messages to me.) You may be saying: "That's just your mind speaking!" You're partly right, for God does speak through the mind. Any thought that comes through the human mind has a certain amount of our own humanness in it, for our minds are only in the natural. However, when I am listening, submitted and surrendered to our Lord, all credit goes to Him for His divine, supernatural inspiration to me. Sometimes when I think back over what He has shared, I say, "Oh, Lord, how beautiful this truth is," and then I wonder what He can possibly say to me tomorrow. Just when I think He has covered every subject in my life, tomorrow comes and He is waiting to shed His truth on yet another cloudy area, or perhaps even a new truth He wants me to know.

There are a few mornings when a little interference appears on the horizon. On those days, it isn't easy to make the connection. It is at this point that I know I must search myself to find out what is causing the interference. I ask myself: "Do I need to ask forgiveness for something or from someone? Is there a sin that I need to confess to God?" After having opened myself to God's cleansing searchlight and repented of any sins He may have shown me, I stand on the promise that God has forgiven me, and has cast those sins away "as far as the east is from the west" (Psalm 103:12). I go to God in the name of Jesus and I expect an answer. I begin praising Him and suddenly the interference is gone. There is no more static and I receive an all-clear signal to go ahead and listen.

There have been times when God has had to repeat His instructions to me more than once. He is so patient, and gentle, and kind. Perhaps I didn't understand, or perhaps I was disobedient. In such cases He has spoken to me again about those areas. He knows our needs and will meet them, if we are willing to listen.

I challenge you to get alone in the morning, at a time when you can be quiet and not rushed...before you become involved in the cares of the day. Show Him you mean business by sacrificing a few extra minutes of sleep for the opportunity to fellowship with Him.

You have probably heard the story of chicken and the pig that lived on a farm. The chicken said, "Let's give the farmer a nice bacon and egg breakfast."

The pig said, "For you it is commitment, but for me, it is sacrifice."

It takes commitment and sacrifice to spend time with the Lord but your blessings will be multiplied.

## Let's get real...

- **Have you ever made a promise to God and not kept it?**
- **Do you realize how important a commitment is in the eyes of God?**
- **Has He ever broken a promise to you?**

Take this moment right now and make a commitment to spend time with Him every day. Put it in your DayPlanner® or on your To Do List! Prepare your heart and your mind for this divine appointment and don't let anything keep you from it. Please consider making this agreement between you and God...and sticking with it. Let me caution you, He is not wild about broken promises but if you show up, so will He and it will be well worth your time.

> Today [date]_____________, I will set aside a special time at ___________ [fill in the hour/AM or PM] when I will have a quiet time and listen for Your voice. I want to learn from you. I need direction for my life and I know You have it. I want to work with You instead of alone. I will come to You because I love You and because I want to get to know you better.
>
> [Name] ________________________________

You will be laying the foundation for a oneness you have never known. Come into His presence with praise and thanksgiving, singing, and Bible reading. I begin each day with Psalm 91, which is my insurance (assurance) policy, and after I read whatever I feel impressed to read, I seek Him.

Never let anyone tell you that learning to know Jesus isn't exciting! I realize that I have only scratched the surface. One morning, He reminded me that it was up to me to determine how fast I would grow in Him and that He would be as big in my life as I would allow Him to be. Many times I have missed an appointment with Him, but when I return He is always there waiting for me. So great is His patience with me! He has been there all the time.

Listening to the Lord is not simply a once-a-day exercise. It should be a minute-by-minute, hour-by-hour, day-by-day, on-going way of life. He is all there is. The world can offer nothing lasting. We must be in it, but not of it, if we belong to Him.

Someone has said that all sin is caused either by rebellion or independence. When we entrust our lives to Him, and become more dependent upon Him, and less dependent upon ourselves or on false gods, we will begin to grow in Him and He in us. Our body, mind, and spirit will then be in one accord. What deep peace follows when we are in harmony with the Lord!

When we allow God's perfect will to be done in our body, soul, and spirit, our triune being moves back into that perfect balance created by Him. It is important that we begin each day by praising Him and asking for His direction and His strength. With Him we are daily conquerors, for He is truly our victory.

I was praying and seeking God concerning a new car. I had prayed and asked Him for a new silver four-door, velour interior, and special model car. However, after checking around, I knew that particular car was not manufactured in that year's model, except in three colors: red, beige and green. How was I to get a new silver car when there was not one to be found? I had checked every dealer in the area…no not one.

God gave me the inward witness that I would get a new silver car of that special make. My head could not understand. So I stood on Proverbs 3:5 which says, "lean not to your own understanding." Mentally, there was no way to figure this one out but in my spirit I knew that I knew that I knew it was going to happen.

One morning in May I was getting ready to have my quiet time with the Lord when I heard that still, small voice say, "Look in the ads in the newspaper," which I promptly did. My eyes fell on an ad from a private party...the exact color, silver, velour interior, four-door, automatic, air, and everything I was looking for. I said to the Lord, "But Lord, I don't want an old car!" When I made the call to inquire, the lady said, "Many calls have come in and several people are on their way to see the car. I don't know if it will still be here when you get here." I had that warm assurance inside that there was no need for me to rush. I praised the Lord as I drove about ten miles.

Upon arriving, I saw the exact car I had seen in the eye of my spirit. But what about the new car I had asked for and God said I could have? I approached the car and found out it had been in storage, it had never even been washed, and had less than one thousand miles! The couple who owned the car had just retired, bought two identical cars and been out of state on vacation in one car for six months. Upon arriving back home, they realized they really had no need for the second car. Praise God! He had everything under control. The couple who had my car were just waiting for me. They were beautiful, committed, and devoted Christians!

Isn't it exciting to hear from God? God is so good! He even cares about cars. He makes ways where there are no ways. His ways are higher than our ways and His thoughts higher than our thoughts.

I think this sixteen year old male resident at House of Hope captured the idea of intimacy very well:

> When we speak of spiritual shift for a generation of people, we are speaking of moving from the soul to the spirit. The only way we can move from the realm of the soul to the spirit is to draw close to God by spending time listening to Him. Then we can go from the natural to the spiritual. Psalm 25:14 says, "The secret of the Lord is with them that fear Him, and He will show them His Covenant" (NKJV).
>
> The word secret is intimate. Intimacy with the Lord is with them who fear Him. As we draw near to God, He will draw near to us. It is in that place of nearness and standing in awe of the Holy God that we grab hold of His covenant. This is the place where we find our "Breakthrough," by spending time with Him.

# Part Two

# The Practical Side of Listening

Chapter 7

# Learning How to Listen

Did you know that God has a telephone number? It's Jeremiah 33:3. "Call unto me and I will answer thee..."

## My Personal Experience...

As you glanced at the index your eyes probably were captured by the title of this chapter...you could hardly wait to quickly read to find out how to listen to the Lord. You want a quick short-cut method. You may have skipped all the preceding six chapters...Dear reader, there are no short cuts. Unless you have the foundation, you can't immediately fly up to the seventh floor without experiencing a fall. Please go back to Chapter 1 and read in sequence. God has an order...and you need to read each chapter to build the foundation for listening.

We must keep God's promise before us at all times knowing that He is going to answer us. We find ourselves needing guidance. We have questions we want answered and we need to hear from God. We look for supernatural guidance through visions, or angels, or a booming voice, but we don't seem to be able to get "in touch." The inner witness is just as supernatural as a vision, yet sometimes we miss God because we are seeking the spectacular. God's Spirit dwells in us. "You are of God, little children, and have overcome them, because He who is in you is greater than he who is in the world" (1 John 4:4 NKJV). We have God's Holy Spirit, which is our inner witness.

If we are Christians, the Holy Spirit bears witness to our spirits, not our minds. There are three voices inside of us and we must be careful not to confuse them:

- There is the voice of our conscience (where the Holy Spirit bears witness to our spirit). This is where we hear the inner witness, impression, or the still, small voice.
- There is the voice of reason, which is the voice of our soul (mind). This is where Satan operates.
- Then there is the voice of self, which comes from self-willed motives or desires.

We need to be aware of the source of the voice we hear.

Has a thought ever been dropped into your mind, which you wanted to remember, but you promptly forgot it because you were too busy to ponder the truth in it? Did you ever stop to think that God was trying to get your attention and tell you something He wanted you to know concerning that thought? Later, when you tried to recall this thought it was gone because of the interruption.

Have you ever been speaking, teaching, preaching, or even just talking with an individual and you heard yourself say something enlightening which you had never thought of before? You said to yourself as you pondered the thought, "Wow that was a profound statement! That's powerful! That wasn't from me! That's a new truth!" You realized immediately that God had given you that thought. Think of the impact and the momentum which that special truth might have had upon you, had you listened to the Lord earlier that day and allowed him to expound and reveal to you even more on that particular subject. When you spoke it later in the day it would have been a double joy, as it was a confirmation of your listening.

Have you ever heard a minister say, "I enjoyed my preaching this morning, for I said things that I heard for the first time?" It really is not an arrogant statement because he was being led and inspired by the Holy Spirit that he was able to convey God's thoughts directly through his mouth. His mind was bypassed. He leaned not to his own understanding. His mouth had spoken before he had realized what he was going to say. God does bypass our imaginations.

How many times have you heard the expression: "Don't jump into water over your head if you don't know how to swim?" This is sound advice for those who operate in the natural realm. Several of the possibilities which may exist if we choose to ignore that safety warning are: We might be able to gasp and flounder our way to safety; embarrassed, we might become the object of the lifeguard's rescue efforts; or, perish the thought, we might drown.

As we operate in the supernatural realm, as "born again" Christians, we must be aware of certain precautions, lest we jump in over our spiritual depths. Do not drop to your knees and expect instant answers from the Lord until you have first checked out the prerequisites for hearing from Him described in the earlier chapters. If you have met those conditions you are now ready to get alone, call on Him and He will answer.

## How To Listen...

Now, before you are ready to learn to listen, to have your own personal breakthrough, there are certain things we need to remember:

- **Bind Satan.** Read James 4:7 (NKJV), "Resist the devil and he will flee from you," or Luke 10:17 (NKJV), "the seventy returned with joy, saying, 'Lord, even the demons are subject to us through Your Name.'"

- **Stay in the Word.** We cannot expect to hear from God if we don't have the Word in us. He speaks to our spirit from the inside out, not from the outside in. (Actually, few people have ever heard Him speak from the outside, with His audible voice.) There are two supernatural forces at work: The Spirit of God and the spirit of Satan. Unless we stay solidly in God's Word, we cannot be sure which voice we are hearing.

- **Align what is heard with the Word of God.** The Bible tells us to try (test the spirits). Spirits, which are vague, general, or condemning, are from Satan. Specific conviction (such as a reminder to pay an overdue bill) comes from God.

"*There is* therefore now no condemnation to those who are in Christ Jesus, who do not walk according to the flesh, but according to the Spirit" (Romans 8:1 NKJV).

## Where Do I Start?

How, exactly, do I start my day listening? This question has been asked of me many times. For the benefit of my readers, here it is. (Your procedure may differ slightly, but if you keep your mind renewed by reading the Word, praying, binding Satan, placing you thoughts under God's captivity, and having a time of praise before listening, He will answer.)

I seek Him early. I begin by reading the Scriptures, Proverbs 8:17 (NKJV) says, "I love those who love me, and those who seek me diligently will find me." As a young child I recall memorizing a poem by Ralph Cushman, which I have on a marker in my Bible. This poem tells of the importance of seeking Him early:

I met God in the morning
When the day was at its best,
And His presence came like sunrise,
Like a glory in my breast.

All day long the presence lingered,
All day long He stayed with me,
And we sailed in perfect calmness
O'er a very troubled sea.

So, I think I know the secret,
Learned from many a troubled way:
You must seek Him in the morning
If you want Him through the day!

I call upon the name of God, letting Him know that I have come into His presence with a surrendered heart and a sanctified mind. Then I bind the voice of the enemy (Satan), with the following verses (remember that the devil hates everyone who is dear to God): "Therefore submit to God. Resist the devil and he will flee from you" (James 4:7 NKJV).

> Jesus said, "I know. I saw Satan fall, a bolt of lightning out of the sky. See what I've given you? Safe passage as you walk on snakes and scorpions, and protection from every assault of the Enemy. No one can put a hand on you. All the same, the great triumph is not in your authority over evil, but in God's authority over you and presence with you. Not what you do for God but what God does for you—that's the agenda for rejoicing" (Luke 10:18-20 The Message).

The tactic of the devil is to throw anything at us that will cause our hearts and minds to stray from one hundred percent attention upon the Lord. The only solution to keeping your heart and mind clean in these evil days is to spend quiet, intimate times daily beholding the beauty of the Lord and being in His presence.

When we disconnect from a daily, intimate fellowship with Him, the chaos of the world creeps in to cause worry and loss of focus. He is our strength and we must labor daily to access and remain in the secret place of the Most High.

Some of you are probably thinking, "The devil never bothers me..." We only need to remind ourselves of the truth which was told to me in jest, "If you're walking down the road and you don't meet the devil walking towards you, you can be pretty sure you're walking with him." Many a note of seriousness has been carried on the wings of a joke.

> "Let the people praise thee, O God; let all the people praise thee" (Psalm 67:3 KJV).

I praise God, knowing that praise binds "...their kings with chains, and their nobles with fetters of iron" (Psalm 149:8 KJV).

The Bible tells us that the Lord inhabits the praises of His people (Psalm 22:3). He sits on the throne of our praises. What better way to have Him inhabit our presence than to praise Him—to grow from the level of asking and thanking into the deeper level of adoring and worshipping Him. God redeemed us so that we might become true worshippers and praisers.

After I have been in the Word, reading several psalms or whatever I choose to read and meditate upon and after

I bind Satan, then I begin praising Him. The next step is to cast down all imaginations and bring all my thoughts under God's captivity. In 2 Corinthians 10:4-5 (NKJV) we read, "For the weapons of our warfare *are* not carnal but mighty in God for pulling down strongholds, casting down arguments and every high thing that exalts itself against the knowledge of God, bringing every thought into captivity to the obedience of Christ."

I remind myself that I must not lean on my own understanding. "Trust in the LORD with all thine heart; and lean not unto thine own understanding. In all thy ways acknowledge him and he shall direct thy paths" (Proverbs 3:5-6 KJV). Then I pray, "Lord, you have invited me to call on You in Jeremiah 33:3 'Call unto Me, and I will answer thee, and show thee great and mighty things which thou knowest not.'"

I remind God of His promise and He answers me. "For I know the thoughts that I think toward you, saith the LORD, thoughts of peace, and not of evil, to give you an expected end. Then shall ye call upon me, and ye shall go and pray unto me, and I will hearken unto you. And ye shall seek me and find *me*, when ye shall search for me with all your heart" (Jeremiah 29:11-13 KJV). It is then that He feeds me with that spiritual manna which is my daily bread!

A word of caution to my readers: I suggest that you not enter into listening to the Lord by asking too many questions. Try to remember, God wants to talk to you. He has been trying to get your attention to tell you things you need to know for a long time. Beware of asking questions that need instant answers, lest we get into an area of the occult. In a time of desperate need, however, God will give us direct answers as we call on Him.

During a vacation my pray partner and I were visiting my parents in North Carolina when she was awakened in the night with intense abdominal pain. After praying, the pain subsided for a while. Throughout the night she was awakened with repeated attacks of pain and after prayer the pain would leave only to return later with greater intensity. Not knowing the cause of the pain was a source of great fear. In desperation she cried out the Lord and said, "Oh, God please tell me what the root of this problem is, so I won't be so afraid." God, with that inner voice, spoke, "You are passing kidney stones."

With great relief we prayed specifically, "Our Father, we thank You for healing our friend and, dear God, we ask You to either dissolve the kidney stones or let them pass as if enclosed in wax. We praise and thank you." Two hours later the stones passed without pain. It was smooth, as if covered with wax. He is always there, listening to our call.

Many times we would like to have instant answers, as did Sandy, but this is not the usual way. There is no time or space with God. He is never too early and never too late. He is always right on time, according to our need.

Several years ago I was asked to share at a prayer meeting on "How to Listen to the Lord." Several of the group have contacted me during the past few years and shared how they have grown closer to the Lord through these experiences of listening.

In the event that any of you may have second thoughts as to whether God really speaks, I would like to share a close friend's experience with you. The following is an excerpt from one of the groups:

> After weeks of coming to meet Him in the mornings and daily receiving a message, either for myself or for someone else, the doubts I had began to leave. I knew these thoughts could not be coming from my mind, for each message was different—a new one each morning—and relating to what my needs (or someone else's needs) would be that day. Yet, even after that breakthrough there still were doubts. I wanted no part of this if it were not from the Lord, so I prayed, "Father, if this is not from You, I ask that you take this away, I don't way to play games in your name, but if it is from You, then allow me a sign to reassure me." In that same still, small voice in my spirit He told me that I would receive a package that day, and that would be His sign to me. In eager anticipation I waited for that package all day, but none arrived.
>
> By the time I got home from work I had convinced myself that the whole thing had been a figment of my imagination and that I was in a pretty mentally unbalanced frame of mind to say the least. The doorbell rang, interrupting these thoughts, and, for some reason I checked the time...7:00 (The Lord's perfect number!). A delivery man, with my package in his hands, stood at the door! I took it from him and instead of opening it, I just held it, for at least fifteen minutes! When I finally opened it, I found it had a present from some friends—a ceramic dove!

Isn't it just like the Lord to send the dove to one of His "present-day doubting Thomases!"

Perhaps you think the above account was a coincidence. Anyone who has ever learned to listen to the Lord knows it was a "God-incidence." Romans 8:28 (NKJV) says, "And we know that all things work together for good to those who love God, to those who are the called according to *His* purpose."

Did you know that when we talk about a "coincidence," we are really mocking God and taking away His power? He is the creator of the universe and knows from beginning to end what will happen, when, why, and how. His orchestration is beyond our comprehension.

*Webster's New World College Dictionary* (Simon & Schuster, 1997) defines coincidence as: **1** the fact or condition of coinciding **2** an accidental or remarkable occurrence of events or ideas at the same time, suggesting but lacking a causal relationship

Does this definition sound like a well-thought out or planned event set into motion by the hand of our omnipotent God? Hardly! With God, you cannot believe in a coincidence. He knew that on this day, you would be reading this book. He prepared you for this. He is molding your heart right now. Nothing is a coincidence with God!

## Let's get real...

- **Have you ever thought of those God-incidences as miracles?**

- **How big and great is your God?**
- **When is the last time God tried to tell you or show you how much He loves you?**

Learning to listen to the Lord is exciting. All the treasures of wisdom and knowledge are hidden in Him. I have discussed the ways to unlock these treasures by sharing with you how to listen to Him so you can have your own personal "Breakthrough." Believe me, your life will be changed.

Chapter 8

# Journaling 101

How you do this is all up to you! There are no formalities in keeping a record of what God speaks into your heart. Just start writing. Forget grammar, sentence structure, and big, fifty-cent words. You are not going to impress anyone. What you write is between you and God.

Below are some of the questions that come up most often.

## What Is Journaling?

Journaling is one of the best ways I have found to write down in my spiral bound notebook what I hear as a result of what happens when I am in the presence of God.

## Why Is It important to Write Down What God Says?

God wants to share the secrets of His heart with you. When I go back in the evening to read what God has spoken during my morning times with Him, my listening is expressed much more beautifully than I could have phrased it in the natural.

## Is the Date Really Necessary?

YES! You are writing your spiritual history with God. Often times when I go back and read from a previous year, I find that what God told me happened just as He said it would. Sometimes revelations that I thought would be impossible or that maybe I had heard wrong proved to be right on target.

> "Write down the revelation and make it plain on the tablets so that a herald may run with it. For the revelation awaits an appointed time; it speaks of an end and will not prove false. Though it linger, wait for it; it will certainly come and will not delay." — Habakkuk 2:2 (NIV)

In the following chapter are some excerpts from my personal notebook where I journal my daily listenings from God.

He sometimes gives me a message accompanied by a picture.

At other times He will quote a scripture to me with an explanation of the meaning.

When I have asked for specifics, He answers and tells me what I need to know.

The answers are not always what I expected.

His thoughts are higher than my thoughts and His solutions are perfect.

Before you begin journaling, you must, MUST wait on the Lord! Your pages will be blank if you don't have this special meeting time with your best Friend. In Isaiah 40:27-31 (The Message) it says,

> "Why would you ever complain, O Jacob,
> or, whine, Israel, saying,
> "God has lost track of me.
> He doesn't care what happens to me"?
> Don't you know anything? Haven't you been listening?
> God doesn't come and go. God lasts.
> He's Creator of all you can see or imagine.
> He doesn't get tired out, doesn't pause to catch his breath.
> And he knows everything, inside and out.
> He energizes those who get tired,
> gives fresh strength to dropouts.
> For even young people tire and drop out,
> young folk in their prime stumble and fall.
> But those who wait upon God get fresh strength.
> They spread their wings and soar like eagles,
> They run and don't get tired,
> they walk and don't lag behind."

From Andrew Murray's book, *Waiting on God* (Christian Literature Crusade, 1999, page 89), he writes, "We must not only think of our waiting upon God, but also of what is more wonderful still, of God's waiting upon us. The vision of Him waiting on us will give new impulse and inspiration to our waiting upon Him. It will give us an unspeakable confidence that our waiting cannot be in vain. If He waits for us, then we may be sure that we are more than welcome, and that He rejoices to find those He has been seeking for....Let us seek even now, at this moment, in the spirit of lowly waiting on God, to find out something of what it means. Therefore will the Lord wait, that He may be gracious unto you. We will accept and echo back the message: Blessed are all they that wait for Him."

## God Will Be Gracious

> "Therefore the LORD will wait, that He may be gracious to you;
> And therefore He will be exalted, that He may have mercy on you.
> For the LORD *is* a God of justice;
> Blessed *are* all those who wait for Him."
>
> —Isaiah 30:18 (NKJV)

He is waiting for you. He is longing for you. He has compassion toward you. He comes running when He hears your voice. He has things He wants to tell you. Get ready to receive!

Chapter 9

# Daily Listenings

## God Is the Pilot

Turn everything over to Me this day. Remember to "be still and know that I am God." I will take charge of each situation, and it will be so easy. Allow me to direct each move of your life, and things will work out perfectly. It's only when you think that you can handle situations independently, without My help, that you run into trouble. Relax. Submit to Me. The going is so easy with Me as your "Director," Pilot, and Guide.

## Contagious Joy

Joy is one of the most "contagious" fruits of My spirit. It is something that everyone desires. I have given you a superabundance to share, and share, and share. People who are afraid of being exposed to it, or "catching" it, should watch out for those "quarantine" signs. People who do not want the joy of the Lord need to segregate themselves from those who are filled with My joy. People who have My joy are highly contagious.

## Praying Specifics

Consider the faucet. You walk up to it when you are thirsty, or when you wish to wash your hands, believing that there is water ready to flow through it. But simply believing this does not cause the water to come rushing out. It is only by reaching out and turning on the faucet handle that water pours forth, in an endless supply, until you are ready to reach out again and turn it off.

The same is true for having your prayers answered. You believe that I will answer your prayers, but it is not until you reach out, being specific in your requests for answers (just as you were specific in your needs for water), that I will answer your prayer requests when you turn on special prayers.

## Total Surrender Leads to Perfect Peace

I give you My Word and I will not go back on it. I have chosen you for a special work. Keep your eyes and ears opened to Me, that I may lead you in all your ways. Mine is a perfect path. Once you have become used to treading it, no other path will satisfy you. Deny yourself and follow Me totally, if you would have perfect peace. I am the Truth, and Light, and the Way. Surrender yourself, and be "sold out" to Me, completely. I will lead, guide, and direct you wherever you go, and in whatever you do, as you keep your eyes on Me.

## Holy Scriptures—Sense of Truth and Freedom

My child, get into My Word. Memorize what I have to say. You shall know the truth, and the truth shall set you free. Don't be confined or imprisoned by what others say concerning my Word. Find out for yourself. As you hear errors in the teaching of others, you will find yourself searching the Holy Scriptures, and your faith will be strengthened by your searching. You will become rooted and grounded in My Word. I sent My Holy Spirit as your teacher. He will teach you by shedding light on the Scriptures as you read. He will speak to you through them so that they will come alive for you. Search out those passages which have imprisoned you, which you do not understand, and I will show the meanings. Listen, and I will make things clear.

## Dying to Self Leads to the Mountaintop

If the process of dying out to self seems slow, or your spiritual growth appears to lie temporarily dormant, have you stopped to consider whether or not there is something at your present level of growth that needs to be dealt with? Are you willing to listen to what I have to tell you, then put that error on the cross for purification? Only then will you undergo another "mountaintop" experience. Self-searching is a daily act. Ask Me to show you that area within yourself that needs to be brought out of darkness. Ask Me to put My holy light on it and purify you...then listen for a few moments, still and quiet, and I will show you what it is and how to deal with it. Be obedient to Me and you will feel a surge of joy flowing through your whole being. There will be such peace that you will know you are reaching another level with Me through Jesus by the power of the Holy Spirit.

## He Supplies Your Needs

As sure as the cold comes to the north in winter, so come I to the aid of My children, in all seasons. I am the man of all seasons, of all needs, and of all promises. If you are in need it's your own fault, for My storehouse is full and running over. You haven't claimed your share, and that share is abundance unlimited.

## God's Love Is Manifested in Your Life

My love, pouring out through you, is more of a witness to those people with whom I have placed you, than a thousands words. It is through the person that I have made you to be, that they will observe and learn more about Me. Your example will speak to their hearts more clearly than listening to sermonettes. Talk is cheap and meaningless, unless it is backed up and proved through daily living.

## Be Still and Know That I Am God

Hearken to My voice. I am in many places where you have not seen Me. Seek Me out. Everything that is pure is of Me. You will discover that I am the good element in all things. I am not diluted. I do not mix with evil. I will not be found in a mixture; I stand out, pure and uncolored. A thing that is shared has been mixed with impurity. I am above contamination. Seek Me with all of your heart and senses, wherever you are. Remember that I love you. Relax in Me today. I am in control. Trust Me, for I have you in the palm of My hand. "Be still, and know that I am God."

## Joy Is Making His Will Your Own

Joy is a part of My nature. I am going to saturate you in My joy today. You can rejoice because you know that nothing can hinder My will in your life because you have asked your will be like Mine. When our wills are in one accord nothing can impede that flow between us. Seek me and you will find Me in every breath you take, in every step, for I am all. I am your source. I will supply.

## Lead Others Into Victorious Living

There appears to be an obstacle course leading to the cross for many committed Christians who are striving daily to follow Me. They cannot seem to get through one tough situation before they encounter another. They realize they are not living a victorious life. Instead, they thrash about in frustration and cry out, "Why, Lord?" You see these people almost daily. I have placed them in your pathway. Pray with them, and intercede for them. I have given you discerning of spirits to know what their needs are, and how to pray for them. Be aware of that friend today who is striving to do what is right. Listen for My discernment. Let Me speak to that person through you, as you pray together.

## Be a Channel for My Blessings

Be on the alert today. I am putting those individuals in your path who have real needs—needs which can only be met by Me, your Savior. I need to use you, for these people do not know to come to Me. They need a physical channel to contact them. They need to see Me working in the life of a person. They need to see joy, peace, faith, and abundance of all things, including love and forgiveness, flowing freely in and around someone who follows Me. Live Me. Love Me. Abide always in Me. I have given you, and will continue to give you, wisdom, knowledge, discerning of spirits, faith, and healing to share with all who are placed in your pathway.

## Wisdom to Guide Others to God

I will give you supernatural wisdom to guide others in those pending decisions which need to be made. My wisdom is yours. Seek Me for it. I'm ready to get the job done when you put forth the effort. Reach out for Me today. There will be many coming to you, in need of Me. Will you guide them, or steer them, in My direction?

Chapter 10

# Meditating Upon His Word

I speak to you about pride. Everyone that is proud in heart is an abomination to Me. "By pride comes nothing but strife, But with the well-advised is wisdom" (Proverbs 13:10 NKJV). Pride disgusts Me. Proud men shall be punished. Pride leads to arguments. Be humble, take advice, and become wise. I have to talk with you about pride—it is an area in your life that needs to be opened up and examined. Keep your eyes on My righteousness, and not on your self-righteousness. Why must you always be right? Do you want to glorify Me or self? To whose glory do you work? It's so easy to commit your way to Me. You don't profit or prosper by what man says. Keep your eyes on Me and man's opinions won't matter. Think about this today. Can't you die a little more to self? It's your decision. Do you want your reward to come from man now or from Me forever?

One day one of the staff at House of Hope spilled coffee on our beautiful carpet. My first reaction was disgust. She had messed up the floor. "The stains probably won't come out," I thought to myself. That was what was in my heart. Later the Lord spoke to me "Greater love hath no man than this..." I should have gotten down in that situation and cleaned it myself. My prayer was this, "Lord, please forgive me. Purify my heart and my actions."

"Commit your works to the LORD, and your thoughts will be established" (Proverbs 16:3 NKJV). Commit your way to Me and then you will succeed. This does not mean just your job, but the total you, at rest, at play, and in all places. When everything is totally surrendered to Me, then you are sure to prosper. There is no failure in or with Me, when one is fully committed. If you should stumble or fall I am always right there to pick you up, brush you off, and give you renewed strength for a new start.

"Wait on the LORD, and keep His way, and He shall exalt you to inherit the land; when the wicked are cut off, you shall see *it*"(Psalm 37:34 NKJV). Don't be impatient for the Lord to act. Keep traveling steadily along His pathway, and in due season He will honor you with every blessing. When you turn to Me in prayer, whether it be for healing of the body, mind, or spirit, don't give up if My answer doesn't come instantly. I must do what is best for you, even if it means keeping you waiting for a little while. A spoiled child wants something the minute he asks for it, but a wise father knows the best time to honor his request. When you ask, know that I have heard you. If what you have asked for is in accordance with My highest and best will for you, I have answered you affirmatively, even though the manifestation of that answer may not appear to you until later. At those periods of waiting, stand on your faith, praise, and give thanks.

The second half of 1 Chronicles 5:20 (NKJV) says, "He heeded their prayer, because they put their trust in Him." I am waiting for you to show Me that you mean business and are serious. I am faithful always to those who have their hope and trust in Me and Me alone. You have cried out to Me for help and I am right by your side. Even though circumstances do not appear favorable, you are not to go on sight but on faith. Don't listen to reasoning of the mind for that is a grave short-coming of man and a very serious confession…I am not a God to mean no when I say yes… you know My promises, claim them, they are all yes.

You asked Me to make your will like My perfect will for you and you are trying to hang on to situations. Just release yourself to Me for I know what is best for you. I see the long-range picture. I know what I have planned for you. Never forget that nothing happens by accident to those who committed to Me. What is happening in your life right now is no accident. It is all part of the plan for you. Just trust Me and don't look to see the past but to the now and trust Me for now and the future. Glorious things and experiences are getting ready to open up for you.

Isaiah 26:3 (NKJV) tells us, "You will keep *him* in perfect peace, *whose* mind *is* stayed *on You,* because he trusts in You." Set your mind to higher things. Don't be affected by your surroundings for they are only temporal. How you react sets examples to the world. Ye are not of the world but are part of the kingdom. You are a child of the King. Now fulfill your role as one of the royal family. Don't let things of this world influence you, but keep your eyes and thoughts stayed on Me and I will keep you in perfect peace. The world loves not My own but rather the worldly…I will strengthen you and supernaturally protect your ears and eyes from the way they act to you and the things they have to say.

I have told you that there are those ways I want you to serve Me as a soldier, an athlete, and as a farmer. If you would serve Me as a soldier you must be armed with My whole armor and especially the sword which is My Word, for you will always be fighting off the enemy (Satan), but he has no power over you in My name. You must fight the good fight and press on to the goal that is promised in Christ Jesus. Press on toward the prize and attain the mark by obeying the rules that I have set down to make you fit for My service. You must daily stay in shape, mentally, emotionally, physically, and spiritually. The last area of serving Me is a farmer. The more you sow, the greater will be your yield. It pleases Me to see My children planting seeds for Jesus. Greater will be the reaping and you will have joy in the harvest. Serve Me in all your ways. I'll direct your every move.

Chapter 11

# Listenings Related to House of Hope

## Concerning House of Hope Staff

This is what God spoke to Sara on May 4, 1985:

"My daughter, it pleases Me to bless your ministry. It pleases Me to unfold the answers to what you have been seeking. It pleases Me to send the right people to you. It pleases Me to pour out My financial blessings on you. There'll never be a financial worry for your ministry. As long as you see to it that each staff member has pure hearts, I'll pour out My Spirit on your ministry and people will drive for miles just to see what is happening, for word will spread of My mighty anointing and move on all the leadership and through you to all the young people. Even adults' lives will be changed as they set foot on the premises. Their hearts will be turned to Me because My power will be so evident there."

"Yes, I will pour out my Spirit on House of Hope and there is no limit to what can happen. Yes, you'll see miracles! And My gifts will be poured out as you keep centered in on Me and My Word. Each day should start with prayer and repentance for I would have all My vessels purified. Each night should end with repentance and prayer and thanksgiving."

"This place is to be set apart for Me as ground where I reign and no one should ever limit My power or deny My mighty move through this ministry."

"There should never be compromise with any issue that comes along or with any person. My Word is to be taught and lived through each one there. Time should be set aside for daily discussions and prayer among the staff. Each problem will be dealt with and the provision will come through Me. Impress upon all the staff to spend quality time daily listening to Me. It is a rule that everyone spend time daily reading and meditating upon My Word and in prayer. Those not willing to conform to listening, study, and prayer will be a hindrance and a stumbling block to the ministry and should be removed from their position. Everyone must be accountable to someone and that accountability must be strictly enforced. Those not willing to be obedient and sacrifice have no place in this ministry, for I will bless and I will reward and you will eat of the good of the land in every area of your lives."

## Listening at the Beginning of Ministry Concerning Money and Trust

February 10, 1985

"I want you to begin giving $500.00 per month. Just give this amount for a six-month period and you will reap rewards which you can't even begin to conceive or understand today. Be obedient and give and I will return to you one-hundredfold. When you are faithful with your giving you can be trusted with greater responsibility (the true riches of heaven). Don't try to reason out your finances or figure your bills, just trust Me with your money. I have given it to you and it pleases Me to see you willing to give it back to Me. I will bless you. I will prosper you and I will enrich your life. I will promote your ministry to the highest level. You will receive the increase in My love and My joy will spill over to thousands upon ten thousands through your ministry."

It was impossible for me to pay my bills and live on $400.00 a month (my total check was $900.00). During that time three people who didn't know about my finances gave or sent money to me, saying, "I felt I was supposed to give you money" and God did provide.

July 31, 1986

"I am pleased with your commitment and obedience giving $500.00 to the ministry. You have proved that you are willing to trust Me in your finances knowing that it is not through your own skills but by trusting Me that I have blessed you and your ministry. You have been faithful in using the gifts I have given you to share your ministry that others might know of what you are doing so they can support you."

"I am pouring out My blessings upon your ministry. I am supernaturally touching hearts to get involved. People will automatically respond to your ministry and won't even stop to think or question why. It is because of My

Spirit drawing them to what you are doing. Be aware and cautious of some who are not supposed to be there."

## Listening Concerning House of Hope Girls

Mighty Warriors

"Eye hath not seen nor ear heard the mighty acts that will come through these teenage warriors. I have an army of young people raised up through House of Hope who will witness to and be used to win other young people unto Me...and they, in turn will, and on and on and on...These young people will be strong and mighty warriors who will be filled with My Spirit and clothed with My armor. They will know their authority in Me and the enemy on the streets of Central Florida will be defeated. House of Hope is the home training ground for warriors."

## Concerning House of Hope Board

November 3, 1985

"Stay tuned to Me and My Word that I may guide you and direct your every step. You must seek My wisdom because there are certain guidelines that you must obey, certain directions and you must follow them. You shall never lack for any good thing. I have already chosen and selected your resources. But I say unto you, do not run ahead, neither lag behind. Spend quality time in seeking Me, you and your board. As you are in one accord, I will lead you step by step into the abundance that I have for you. Wherever there is indecision or disagreement, do not make a decision until you seek Me and come to total agreement. I will answer. I will provide and I will bless, and again I say, do not settle for an answer when there is even one who is negative. For I will give that inner witness to all to move in the same direction."

## Two Months Before the House of Hope Doors Opened

June 21, 1985

"The thoughts have come into your mind...'Am I sure 30th Street is where we're supposed to be?' Yes, My child, this is to be where your headquarters are. This is to be your runaway facility. This is where your main office is to be established. There is going to be an enlarged extension at another site. There is no limit to what I can do. I will be as big as your vision—for I will pour out My Spirit upon your ministry as you seek Me for guidance and purity of all the vessels that are part of this ministry. Be very selective in your staff—for there are Christians...but there are anointed Christians that I have preordained for this work. Don't stop short of My very best, the workers I have anointed, just because others may seem more available. I will give you My approval on your staff and you will know when there is that certainty in your spirit. I will confirm the right selections through others that you respect spiritually."

"There will be smoke screens—people will come who are impressive and will seem just perfect for the job by outward signs, but I will cause you to discern the person's spiritual strength and recognize their inner man of the heart. Call on Me. Some others say no, but I will say yes."

A major aspect of our program at House of Hope is teaching the girls to listen to the Lord. Here is an example of a word from the Lord received by one of our precious girls:

> "You are special to Me. Don't think you are not like the rest in My eyes. You are all equal. You were doing so good. Don't let evil back into your spirit. You know every time you try to live for Me, something gets in the way. Doesn't that tell you something? Don't worry about the future all the time. Think about now. Put all other things aside. Your life is planned and will go as I plan. Just remember to live in righteousness, not evil. You will leave the program in **My time.** Don't dwell on the past and forget about the future. Just keep on like you were and you will see. We all fall, sometimes worse than others. But I will pick you up. All this you are learning is real, not fake. Pay more attention and you will be surprised. Seek Me! I am here for you, Billie Jo, in times of trouble and laughter."
>
> —Received by Billie Jo (Billie Jo graduated on 1/20/89 from our program—in His time!)

"I am drawing together quality men and women to band together...to love...to commit...to sacrifice... to pray...to become one in the Spirit, to undergird the ministry at House of Hope. There is no outside force that can conquer...for I have set this ministry apart as a special work...as a beacon of light...to give hope...to change and heal the hurting and brokenhearted. I will send those to you I choose. Be sensitive to their spirits. For I would not have just anyone be in your ministry. Many will come and many will be led away...for I have called a special people to work with House of Hope...a people who are willing to sacrifice...to sell out to Me. A people who can see beyond the storms, beyond the shipwrecked lives of those I send to you. A people who are not threatened by circumstances, a people who don't give up when the going gets rough...people who truly want to serve Me...to forsake all and follow Me...a people willing to trust Me when they are discouraged...to turn to Me...to My Word...the source of their strength...a people committed to Me and to each other...people who are always there for one another to pray and encourage...these are the kind of people I am bringing into your ministry."

When God speaks to me or gives me a vision, He never gives me the whole picture at one time. That would probably be too frightening and I wouldn't have to exercise my faith to believe for what God had shared with me.

I shared what God had said with four friends who were excited and expectant for we only had $200.00 among us. God told me the two things: The ministry was to be a faith ministry—we were always to be debt free. The second thing was that it would be a requirement for parents to be involved.

When God told me to start House of Hope in 1985, I thought we would only have eight or ten girls and live happily ever after. A few years later, He said to increase to twenty five girls. Ten years later, He said it was time to expand our territory to move to another location.

In the meantime, He was preparing House of Hope Orlando to be the national training headquarters for National House of Hope. Today we believe that there will be a House of Hope within driving distance of every major city in America.

By the way, today we have a debt-free, ten acre campus with fourteen buildings. We don't turn away the poor, and it is a requirement that parents become an integral part of their teen's program and healing process.

## The Roots in our Lives

Just recently my older brother and I shared some "growing up" stories. There was one that painted a great picture how we sometimes run ahead and are brought to our knees because we did not hear from God.

One of our earliest memories was watching my Dad and helping him work in his vegetable garden. Usually he would have a mule to assist in the plowing. We talked about how sometimes we are like a young mule—strong and able but not having the experience of getting a job done.

My brother shared about seeing Dad's young mule hitched to a plow—breaking ground that had not been previously plowed. The mule was going strong until it hit a stump or big root. It brought the mule to its knees. It didn't take many "roots" to break that mule. Then when he felt the least bit of resistance, he'd slow down. That is a great picture for our lives. We don't take time to stop to listen until we are brought to our knees. The moral of this story is: When we hit a root in our life or feel resistance, we need to slow down and seek the Lord. He is always right there waiting.

# Let's get real...

- Are you ever mulish?
- Have you ever gotten ahead of the Holy Spirit? Even Mary and Joseph went on and did their own thing and left Jesus behind in the Temple. They had to turn around and go back and find him (Read Luke 2:39-52).
- How much emotional, physical, and spiritual pain do you need to endure before you realize that God is trying to get your attention?

Chapter 12

# Hearing With New Ears

Communication seems to be the most serious problem in the "breakdown" of the family...people don't know how to listen...and the most serious problem with us Christians is that we don't really communicate with God because we don't spend much time with the Lord.

In a recent survey, the average Dad spends less than two minutes per day in active eye-to-eye listening to his children...without competition from the TV or newspaper. The average Mom spends less than five minutes a day actively listening to her children. And we wonder why we are having family problems! The answer is quality time.

I could share with you all kinds of do's and don'ts and skills for parents and teenagers, but today I want to share on something more important, and that is establishing a listening relationship that will last forever. God wants to intervene...we need divine intervention.

The root of family problems is spiritual. When parents have no relationship with Jesus their family is out of divine order. We must set the example.

How many of us spend time alone with Jesus? Focused time...one-on-one, with no distractions...listening to his voice...enjoying His presence...allowing Him to intervene in your life!

We can't depend on the President to hear from God for us...We can't depend on our minister, or our friends, to tell us what God wants us to know. We must have a personal "one-on-one" relationship with Jesus Christ if we're to be victorious warriors in the end times. That means spending quality time with Him, and being able to hear his voice.

In John 10:27 (The Message) Jesus says, "My sheep recognize my voice. I know them, and they follow me. I give them real and eternal life." If you are not one of His sheep please take the time to become one of His flock.

In Psalm 32:8 He told us He would guide us and direct the paths we should go. He's trying to get our attention. He wants us to listen as we've never listened before.

He's the same Jesus who spoke to me sixteen years ago and told me to start House of Hope with $200.00 and five people praying! He told me to bring healing and restoration to families, to rescue hurting teenagers from the muck and mire, darkness, desperation, destruction, despair, and even death of our society. He's still speaking to me today, giving me direction day-by-day.

The last time I talked with Him (which was throughout the writing of the original and the revision) He told me not to worry, to cast all my cares on Him and He will continue to provide steady guidance. All we need to do is show ourselves faithful and spend quality time listening to His voice.

## Let's get real...

- **Do you ever feel far away from God?**
- **Have your prayers hit an impasse?**
- **Ever find yourself asking, "Where is God?"**

I want to share a story about two brothers who were always getting into trouble, who were such problems, so incorrigible and unruly, that they were sent to their pastor to see if He could do anything with them. He took the older boy into his office and sat the younger one in the outer office. The Pastor asked the older boy, "Son, where is God? Where is God? Where is God?"

The boy dashed out of the office, grabbed his little brother, and said to him, "Let's get out of here quick! God is missing and they're blaming us!"

Seriously, we need to ask ourselves if God is missing in our lives today, who is to blame?

For those in the ministry, listening to the Lord is a matter of life and death—that is, if we're to be who God created us to be. God is calling you and me to a more serious listening relationship with Him.

I wonder just how many of us are not walking in God's true calling because we haven't heard His voice and can't follow His perfect will for our lives.

Won't it be sad when we stand face to face with Jesus and He says, "Sara, Alfred, Sandy, Aaron, Virginia...I had so much more for you...but you never took time to really seek Me, spend the time with Me...and obey."

Tonight I'm praying for divine intervention in your life.

I want to challenge you to hear Jesus knocking at the door to your heart. He's saying to you and me, "Behold, I stand at the door and knock. If anyone hears My voice and opens the door, I will come in to him and dine with him, and he with Me" (Revelation 3:20 NKJV).

Do you want to learn how to let Him in? He is not going to pull the door open. You have to open the door for Him and invite Him inside. At that point, you can spill your guts and start talking to Him like never before. While He already knows what you have done, what you are doing, and what you are going to do, He wants to hear from you. He will make His presence known to you in mighty and powerful ways. Just open the door!

How much we hear from God is determined by how much quiet time we spend with Him. It doesn't seem like many people that I talk with take time to listen. Most people in our modern world don't hear because their schedules are too busy to hear from God. If God doesn't leave a

Voicemail, or if He doesn't send them an email or a fax, God doesn't get an opportunity to speak to them. Jeremiah 33:3 (God's phone number).

Every day I realize more and more how vital it is for me to listen to the Lord. There's no one here who is spending too much time with Jesus!

We need to set aside time when we can be quiet, get alone with God and learn His will for us. David said in Psalm 46:10, "Be still, and know that I am God" (NIV).

I've found I have to make time to listen every day. Each of us is given the same twenty-four hours a day. We choose how we spend our free time.

Spending time with God is like spending time with a friend. We don't ever get to know God if we do all the talking and never take the time to listen to what He wants to say to us. If we do all the talking, we don't ever really get to know Him.

God always redeems the time I spend with Him. Somehow I get more accomplished when I give Him first priority. (I meet God in the morning.)

I have heard some people say that they can only hear from God if they are on their knees in prayer in their bedroom, or at the altar of a church, but some of my best listening times are when I'm in the car alone. Many times I reach for a yellow pad to write down as I'm driving what He's saying to me.

There are many ways the Lord speaks to us. God speaks through His word, through dreams and visions, through prophecy, through an audible voice, through mature believers, and through that "still, small voice." God always speaks to us through His Word. God's written word is our final authority! Period!! That is why we need to know what God's Word says. In Matthew 22:29-33 (The Message) Jesus verbally slaps the Pharisees. They know the words but they don't know the Word.

> Jesus answered, "You're off base on two counts: You don't know your Bibles, and you don't know how God works. At the resurrection we're beyond marriage. As with the angels, all our ecstasies and

> intimacies then will be with God. And regarding your speculation on whether the dead are raised or not, don't you read your Bibles? The grammar is clear: God says, 'I am—not was—the God of Abraham, the God of Isaac, the God of Jacob.' The living God defines himself not as the God of dead men, but of the living." Hearing this exchange the crowd was much impressed.

I want to talk about the most common way God speaks personally if we allow Him, and that's through His still, small voice. For those of you who have never heard God speak in that still, small voice, there is no audible sound. It comes from within. God has the best communication system going. It beats anything on the market today and is better than AT&T or Bell South. He gives us unlimited time! It is direct spirit to Spirit. God is a spirit and He delights in bypassing our minds and speaking directly to our spirits.

Some people think that when God speaks to them they have to see flashing lights and hear bells or whistles and sirens! Many people have heard the voice of the Lord and never realized who they were hearing.

You'll hear people say things like, "something told me to pick up the phone and call that person…I can't explain it, but when I called they told me how happy they were that I had called…They'd been sick and needed someone to pray with them." That "something" was, of course, the voice of the Lord. The devil won't tell you to call desperate people just when they need your help and your prayers.

It's time to stop calling God "something" or a "sudden impulse" or a "strange feeling came over me" and learn to recognize God's voice!!

One day I was praying and that still, small voice gave me the name "Frances" and told me to pray for that person. Many times when writing my prayer list the lord will still give me the name of someone I don't know.

Driving to work one day I felt prompted by the Lord to pray for my brother, Paul. I prayed a prayer of safety and protection. You may never know the outcome of these prayers but your obedience has stirred something in the supernatural. By speaking to us through His still, small voice, God can communicate His will to us anywhere and at any time. He can speak to us when we are in the midst of a large crowd or in a great crisis or alone...if we will just stay tuned to Him.

When I really urgently need to hear from God for a special need or decision I get alone with Him, usually fast a day or so, until I get the answer. He does exceedingly, abundantly beyond what I could ever image. Later, I read back what He said and it is so beautiful! But sometimes there is chastening. One sentence from God to me personally is worth one hundred sermons!

He is always there when we call upon Him!

Did you ever lose something and, after searching for hours, and maybe even days, you finally (in desperation) sat down and said: "Oh, Lord where could that thing be?" Suddenly He drops the answer into your mind? That answer is his still, small voice. You immediately go and look and there it is! And you think: "if only I had called on the Lord first, think of all the time I would have saved!"

I believe we're living the most exciting time in history!!!

God does have a special plan for each one of us Christians. The big key is: We need to know what the Spirit of God is saying to us.

He has a plan and that plan is for us to trust Him.

God is calling you and me right now to be set apart. We are to be His end-time leaders, intercessors, warriors, and people who don't fear. We are to be a people who walk in peace because we trust Him. We are to be the people who are calm when the rest of society panics.

That doesn't mean we don't have to face some suffering. It does mean that! But we have a promise that even in our most difficult times, He will be right there with us, holding up hands, if only we'll listen and be obedient.

In John 16:33 (NKJV) Jesus said, "These things I have spoken to you, that in Me you may have peace. In the world you will have tribulation; but be of good cheer, I have overcome the world."

In closing, many people ask me how I go about listening to the Lord, how I get into His presence. I'll tell you simply what I do. Personally, I listen to the Lord by:

1. **Binding Satan** (James 4:6-7) – Humble yourself before God, resist the devil and he will flee.

2. **Placing all my thoughts under His captivity** (2 Cor. 10:5) – Casting down imaginations (2 Cor. 10:3-5).

3. **Calling on Him** (Jer. 33:3).

Sometimes I read scriptures, sometimes I praise Him and ask what He wants to say to me. Sometimes He tells me the meaning of a scripture and sometimes it's a picture. Sometimes it's a page or two on what He wants me to know. I've missed a lot of appointments, but He never has!

Chapter 13

# Being Intimate With God

There are many spiritual battles we engage in throughout our Christian life, but I believe the greatest one is the battle for intimacy with the Lord. If we want a fruitful life in the kingdom we must learn how to be intimate. The character and nature of Jesus is formed in us through intimacy with Him (spending quality time alone with Him). It is no wonder that so many things distract us.

Intimacy is the battlefield. This is the area the enemy desires to steal more than anything! If he can steal our intimacy with the Lord, he gets everything. The battle for intimacy is not a one-time fight. It is constant. The enemy will use anything he can to distract us: condemnation, busyness, lack of focus, and distractions with other priorities, such as telephone calls, meetings, TV, and on and on. We must learn to fight against or say no to all of these distractions.

Let's talk about why God wants to be intimate and speak to us today—because He loves us.

He wants to:

- Fellowship with us,
- Give us direction,
- Help us make decisions,
- Comfort and reassure us, and
- Sometimes He needs to chasten us to get us back on the right track.

Throughout the Bible God has always spoken to His people. He spoke to:

- Abraham—Direct revelation
- Joseph—Dreams
- Moses—Laws and 10 Commandments
- Prophets—"Thus sayeth the Lord"
- Angels—Birth of Jesus
- Saul of Tarsus—"Saul, Why do you persecute Me?"
- Today through His Holy Spirit—"The still, small voice"

God will never tell us to do anything contrary to His Word.

What are some ways God uses to get our attention if we refuse to be intimate and not listen?

- Sometimes through someone else
- Unanswered prayers
- Drying up of finances
- Problems at work
- We become restless
- Through dreams

- Unusual circumstances
- Prophetic word

When we are intimate with someone we communicate. “Communication” seems to be the most serious problem in the “breakdown” of the family. People don’t how to listen to each other or to be intimate. The most serious problem with us Christians is we get so busy that we don’t really take time to communicate with each other or with God.

Parents wonder why they are having family problems! The answer is, “We must take quality time to be intimate and to listen to each other.” Love is spelled T-I-M-E.

Today I want to share on the importance of establishing an intimate and listening relationship with Jesus that will last forever. God is wanting to intervene…We need “divine intervention.” How many of us regularly spend time alone with Jesus? Do you have focused time, one-on-one, with no distractions, with no TV—listening to His voice, enjoying His presence, and allowing Him to intervene and make a difference in your life?

We can’t depend only on prophets, our minister, or our friends to tell us what God wants us, individually, to know. We must have a personal, one-on-one relationship with Jesus Christ if we’re to be victorious warriors in these end times. That means spending quality, intimate time with Him, being able to hear His voice, and writing down what He says.

In John 10:27, Jesus says, “My sheep hear My voice….” If you’re one of His sheep say, “Baah, Baah!!”

After teens have been in the residential program for several months and begin to find their identity in Christ, they begin to accept love, receive healing, and start on the road to their destiny. Much of this is accomplished through their quiet times as they listen to the Lord.

Before a teen graduates from House of Hope, he or she is required to teach during one of Tuesday morning campus-wide chapel services. When they reach this phase in the program, it is amazing to see how tall they stand, and how they are able to look others in the eye. My heart is always happy as I listen to them speak from the measure of faith that has developed in their hearts.

I want to share with you part of what one teen shared recently. Nathaniel was in and out of a detention center for robbery, drugs, etc. His family did not have time for him and by the time he was thirteen, he was virtually on his own.

He was supposed to go to a lock-down facility (juvenile prison) and to be put on probation until he was nineteen years old.

However, the judge had mercy on his mother and ordered Nate into House of Hope, Orlando. Five months after being in the program, he accepted Jesus Christ as his personal Savior. He now has hope and faith. His probation officer could hardly believe his eyes when he saw Nate. The many changes in him were dramatic. Here is part of what Nate shared:

## My Identity

I am a branch that grows from the Vine (Jesus Christ).
My mission is to rise as high as I can, as long as I can,
Bearing as much fruit as I can along the way.
No one can stop me because I am connected to the Vine.
If you cut me, I'll grow longer, stronger, and faster.
If you put something in my way,
I'll grow over it, around it, and sometimes even under it.
Or, I'll find a crack and go through it.
I'll embrace every obstacle along the way.
Using each one as a rung on a ladder.
Each triumph gives me the strength I need to climb.
Each adversity gives me the hunger and courage I need
To prepare for the next level.
This is Who I am.
This is my Destiny,
Because I 'm connected to the Vine.

How could a teenage, troubled boy learn all this?

He embraced the quiet times with the Lord and learned to listen to His voice. Hope and faith are fruit that grow in Nate as a result of being connected to the Vine. They are equal and vitally important in his spiritual journey.

Many years ago, Mary Martin sang a song in the Broadway musical South Pacific with the following words: "I'm stuck like a dope with a thing called hope, and I can't get it out of my heart." At House of Hope, these are our sentiments. We embrace all hurting teens with this kind of attitude. We are stuck with hope in our hearts for each one. Hope and faith account for our huge success rate in reconciling and restoring teens to their parents.

If you're going through troubled waters today and things look hopeless, remember, "Hope deferred makes the heart sick, but a longing fulfilled is a tree of life" (Proverbs 13:12 NIV). I want to encourage you to get alone with God. Cry out to Him! Listen for His answer. Only He can fill the longing in your heart.

Find a promise in God's word that applies to your situation and trust God for the answer. He has granted to us His precious and magnificent promises, so that by them you may become partakers of His divine nature (2 Peter 1:4).

Your longing will be fulfilled<br>—if you don't give up!

## Chapter 14

# The House of Hope Story

The direction and guidance of House of Hope has come as a result of many people listening to the Lord and acting on what He has told us.

For fifteen years I taught emotionally handicapped teenagers in the Orange County school system, in junior high school and a state juvenile detention center. The situation seemed hopeless for teenagers. They would come and go with no solutions and no answer to their problems, and they would repeat their negative behavior. There seemed to be no lasting help for these desperate young people. We were not allowed to teach life-changing principles based on God's Word.

During one of my early morning prayer times, God spoke to me in His still, small voice and said, "Sara, your ministry is going to branch out into a new direction." One year later, that new direction became House of Hope, a Christian home for hurting runaway/throw away teenagers. I shared this vision with the Board of Directors of Fellowship of Faith Ministry, Inc., and their hearts were touched. This would be our opportunity to teach Christian principles to teenagers, help heal their hurts and minister Jesus Christ to help change the lives of young people and their parents permanently!

We had no money, no house, no facility, but I had a vision and knew God was directing me. One day as I was praying and asking God about a location, the name of a lady who owned a Bible bookstore came strongly to my mind and I felt impressed to call her. I asked if she might know a location for a home we could use for teenagers. She said she had a friend who was getting ready to sell two houses, a garage, and three lots. After seeing the site and talking with the lady, we immediately knew this was to be the future House of Hope. The first price quoted was $117,000. That seemed like a million dollars to us because we had no money—but I still had a dream! Since the owners were Christians we asked if they would pray about a final price.

In the meantime, someone suggested we write a grant request to the Edyth Bush Foundation. The person went on to say, "But they never give to Christian groups only the Arts, Sciences, and Theater." I had no experience with grant writing but several of us, once again, asked God for guidance and, after much prayer, submitted a grant requested of $95,000 in matching funds. At this point I had no idea why God told us to ask for $95,000.

The property owners called in a few days (not knowing about the amount of our grant request) and said, "We've decided to let you have the property for $95,000!" Now we knew and rejoiced believing we would get the grant. By faith I said, "Fine, we'll take it." They prepared for the closing but we still had no money! Two weeks before the closing date, I received a letter from the Edyth Bush Foundation saying, "We are happy to announce that you will receive your request of $95,000!" God is so good...He is never late!

Sometime later I was a guest on a television program, which followed an interview of Charley Reese, a nationally syndicated columnist of the *Orlando Sentinel*. He was so impressed that we refused government funds that he asked if he might write an article about the House of Hope. The article was scheduled to appear in the *Sentinel* on May 29, 1985, the same day that President Reagan would visit Epcot Center, in Orlando, for only three hours at their dedication. We prayed that somehow, in spite of his busy schedule, the President would read the article. Once again God answered our prayer. The President read it, wrote a letter of congratulation and encouraged the community to get involved in free enterprise. He included a $1,000 check from his personal account. Another God-incident!

The community began to become aware of what we were doing and the great need for this unique home. Carpenters donated materials and labor and plumbers, electricians, painters, and repairmen, etc., rallied to God's calling. One house had a large hole in the roof. Early one morning when I arrived, five men were on top of the house building a new roof! These men were unknown to us but known to God.

Our doors to House of Hope opened August 22, 1985. Just exactly what we needed: beds, furniture, appliances, dishes, linens, pots and pans, clothing, etc., came from individuals, organizations, and churches.

Shortly after we moved in, we found that the carpet in one house was full of fleas! An exterminator came and told us that the rug was infested with fleas and eggs, which would be impossible to take care of in one trip, and each visit would cost us $40.00. There were no funds for this. When we walked into the house our legs were peppered with fleas! And the girls were coming the next day! In desperation I felt impressed to use my authority as a Christian (Luke 10:19) and went through each room, commanding every flea to leave. Since that day there has never been another flea at House of Hope! Praise the Lord! We'll never put the exterminators out of business, but God knew we had a need.

We needed some office furniture and chairs. One day as I looked in the yellow pages one name seemed to stand out. The next day while looking at newspapers ads, the same name seemed to leap from the page. I called that number and introduced myself. The lady practically shouted—she had been trying to get in touch with me for two days. She went on to say if it had not been for our twenty-four-hour prayer hotline she would not be alive today. If one of our prayer counselors had not prayed with her she would have committed suicide. Now she has hope through Jesus Christ. The grateful lady who happened to own a furniture store told me, "Come down right now and pick out what you need."

A lady came to House of Hope to volunteer her services to clean and wax the floors. She had felt the Lord leading her to House of Hope. She would need a buffer. At that time we had very few phone calls. At that moment the phone rang and a voice on the other end asked us if we needed a buffer! What confirmation! This precious lady has been with us ever since.

One night the girls prayed for a color television. The very next day a stranger delivered a beautiful color television. And the Lord's blessings continue to flow! The girls loved grilled cheese sandwiches for lunch and for a while we had no cheese. The girls decided they had better pray! Two days later a fifty-pound hoop of cheese arrived at the door!

On October 28, 1985, our part-time bookkeeper let me know that it was time to pay the bills. We owed $6,000 in bills and we only had $5,700. We agreed together in prayer (Matthew 18:19) and believed that God would touch someone's heart to give. Two days later a letter arrived from someone in New York State. You guessed it! There was our check for $300! From fleas to finances, God cares about the hurting teenagers at House of Hope!

We have a beautiful staff of born-again Christians and many indispensable volunteers. Our A.C.E. (Accelerated Christian Education) School offers a high school diploma. The A.C.E. program is a Christian alternative program to public school education.

The number of teenagers who desperately need this facility staggers the imagination. House of Hope is a faith ministry, totally dependent upon the local businesses, corporations, church support, and caring people who have a heart for helping hurting teenagers.

We maintain a maximum capacity of twenty five girls and six boys in our program because we want each teen to get the individual attention and home atmosphere they so desperately need and may have never received before.

Our vision is to see other Houses of Hope spring up across the nation. To that end we hold training seminars to teach others how to start one in their area. Many other Houses of Hope have already begun. Today House of Hope Orlando is the model for National House of Hope. There are dozens of Houses of Hope across America patterned after House of Hope Orlando.

Reconciling the family is key at House of Hope. Our goal is to return each teen home to a healthy and loving relationship with the family. We, therefore, expect all parents and other family members to participate in once-a-week individual counseling and a weekly parenting class.

Outpatient counseling is available for girls and their families who are not in the program. We also offer counseling to others in the community.

At House of Hope we minister to body, soul, and spirit. We have a full size, fully equipped gymnasium with exercise equipment and aerobic classes and intramural games. We have classes on etiquette, health, social graces, and beauty.

Our goal at House of Hope is to prevent hundreds of hurting young people from being destroyed on the streets in our community. We want to protect them from our drug-altered, child-abusing, sex-for-sale society where children are being exploited, facing horrors, and experiencing defeat. Social agencies and institutions try to help teenagers, but young people continue to desperately yearn for love and a sense of being wanted. There's no lasting help when Jesus Christ cannot be shared. Streets and institutions don't "tuck them in" at night, but we do at House of Hope. What a privilege that God counted us worthy to love, serve, and help hurting teenagers, most of whom tell us they would not be alive today had it not been for House of Hope.

Designed to be an anchor to hurting teenagers drifting in troubled waters, House of Hope proves an atmosphere of love...Christian love...through Christian counseling and intervention techniques to reconcile and restore the family. Our Christian staff is well qualified to provide assistance in meeting each teenager's need. This ministry has a ripple effect, for not only are the girl's lives touched but also their families, friends, and everyone whose life touches theirs.

Sir Edmund Burke, noted British statesman, said something to the effect of, "A sure way for evil to triumph is for good men to do nothing." House of Hope is doing something. We are changing lives—the lives of our young people—our most precious natural resource and America's future.

The Lord impressed upon me to include a prayer for those who may feel:

- unworthy
- guilty
- unforgiven
- inadequate
- or perhaps uncommitted.

Maybe there is an area in your life where you need God to help you to be an overcomer. Maybe it is something that no one but you and God need to know about.

If you are in one or more of the above categories, perhaps you would like to make the prayer on the following page your own personal confession.

Dear God:

You told me in Romans 10:9 that if I would confess with my mouth that Jesus is lord, and if I would believe in my heart that you raised Jesus Christ from the dead, that I would be saved. I make these confessions now.

I confess that I have sinned the following ways (list them below):

________________________________________

________________________________________

________________________________________

________________________________________

________________________________________

________________________________________

________________________________________

________________________________________

Thank you that You are faithful to forgive me and cleanse me from all sins (1 John 1:9).

Thank you that You have forgiven me as far as the east is from the west (Psalm 103:12).

Thank you that this means You will no longer remember my sins.

Now Jesus, I open the door of my heart to receive You as my Savior and my Lord. I want to be more like You each day.

One further thought, Lord...I ask You to baptize me with Your Holy Spirit for I need your power to be an overcomer in your end-time army.

In Your precious name, Jesus, Amen

________________________________________

(Your signature)

________________________________________

(Date)

Epilogue

# Where Do We Go from Here?

## Listenings from Tuesday, December 28, 2006

"As you spend time with Me, I will unfold My plans to you. There is a great and powerful anointing upon you. To whom much is given, much is expected. I have called you to help humanity through House of Hope but I have a greater calling for you. I have called you to use these Houses of Hope as a springboard for my mighty power and miracles to be performed. These Houses of Hope are not just to rescue teens and families. They are places for My Glory to be revealed with signs, wonders, and miracles which will be performed. This network of Houses of Hope will spread across the World and will be instrumental in bringing revival. Then, in My authority, will they recognize the uniqueness of this movement and will be in awe of My mighty move. People in authority will give their lives to Jesus and be filled with the Holy Spirit through House of Hope Ministry. I will address, select, and initiate this great move. I will send the right people to be your armor bearers as you lead this great move across the world."

"Prepare yourself by spending time with Me. I have called, equipped, ordained, and am making the way for this mighty move through you. I am already putting the people around you...in the proper places to be your support. I will make it happen. I've given you faith to make it happen."

## Listenings from Sunday, December 31, 2006

"I have especially selected the staff at House of Hope to be an example to the world...to be an example to the body of Christ with all the gifts in operation. I would have each one flow to the fullest in the fits and calling I have ordained. House of Hope is to be an example to the body of Christ as to how the Body of Christ is to operate. Each part of the body is important. I have given you different gifts for different purposes. Find your gifts and flow to the fullest. If one member doesn't flow it will throw the body out of alignment. You are to be a ministry and body of excellence."

During the past year I went to a chiropractor who showed me an x-ray of my spine. My body was out of alignment with my head. As a result I was in pain. I needed an adjustment. And then I was reminded of what the Lord had said to me earlier. A ministry of excellence must be in alignment with the head...Jesus Christ.

# Let's get real...

- Do you need a spiritual adjustment?
- Are you searching for more of something that seems to be just out of your grasp?
- Are you prepared to stand before Him face-to-face?
- Will you recognize His voice on that final day?

While I personally do not know exactly what the future holds for me and for House of Hope, there is One who does. I pray that you will come to know Him, hear His voice, and step out of your comfort zone to do great and mighty things for His kingdom.

# Do You Have a Passion To Help Hurting Teens?

Would you like to learn more about starting a House of Hope? Our goal is to have a House of Hope within two hundred miles of every major city in the United States. Big goal? Yes, but there are big problems that our teens face today! These homes for troubled teens are based on successful counseling and education programs that model after the House of Hope in Orlando, Florida. There are new Houses of Hope in many states now and the number is growing.

**To learn more about House of Hope and to attend a training seminar, please contact:**


Sara Trollinger
House of Hope
P.O. Box 560503
Orlando, FL 32856
407-843-8686
Email: houseofhopesara@aol.com
Visit our Web site: www.nationalhouseof hope.org

# Other Books by Sara Trollinger

A Guidebook for Parents: ***Unglued & Tattooed:*** How to Save Your Teen from Raves, Ritalin, Goth, Body Carving, GHB, Sex, and 12 Other Emerging Threats (LifeLine Press, 2001)

***Unglued, Tattooed & Renewed***: Compelling stories from teens whose lives have been drastically changed (2003)

**To order any of these books,**
**please contact House of Hope:**

407-843-8686
Email: houseofhopesara@aol.com
Visit our Web site: www.nationalhouseof hope.org